"A distillation of the experiences of a pioneer in amplifying the voice of the customer. Anyone who wants to understand the world of consumer-generated media should read Pete Blackshaw's book."
—*James L. Heskett, Baker Foundation Professor, Emeritus,*
Harvard Business School

"The only way this book could provide a more substantial take on consumer-generated media is if Blackshaw allowed his readers to write it themselves." —*Dave Balter, CEO, BzzAgent*

"Powerful and compelling. [Blackshaw's] book lays out a straightforward road map for companies and brands to follow to re-engineer the way they listen, respond, and engage with today's empowered consumers." —*Linnea Johnson, Director of Consumer Services, Unilever*

"Highly readable . . . Proves the importance and value of credibility, and delivers practical advice on how to earn credibility through authentic relationship management."
—*Jim Boyce, President of Communications, Technology, Media,*
Entertainment, and Canada Groups, Convergys Corporation

"Provides frank insight . . . on how marketers and consumer-affairs professionals can more effectively navigate this new landscape. Net result: [*Satisfied Customers Tell Three Friends*] helps me stay on top of my game."
—*Tom Asher, Head of Consumer Relations North America,*
Levi Strauss & Co.

"This book is far less about technology or 'the next cool thing' than very simple truths and principles—earning trust and building credibility through listening, responsiveness, dependability, and performance. BBB has served as the marketplace voice for these principles for nearly 100 years, and Pete puts them all into a contemporary mission-critical context."
—*Steven J. Cole, President and CEO, Council of*
Better Business Bureaus, Inc.

"A practical how-to guide—filled with great examples and stories—on how to build your brand authentically in today's world."
—*Tony Hsieh, CEO, Zappos.com*

Satisfied Customers Tell Three Friends, Angry Customers Tell 3,000

Running a Business in Today's Consumer-Driven World

PETE BLACKSHAW

DOUBLEDAY

NEW YORK LONDON TORONTO SYDNEY AUCKLAND

ⅅD

DOUBLEDAY

PUBLISHED BY DOUBLEDAY

Copyright © 2008 by Pete Blackshaw

Published in the United States by Doubleday, an imprint of The Doubleday Publishing Group, a division of Random House, Inc., New York.

www.doubleday.com

DOUBLEDAY is a registered trademark and the DD colophon is a trademark of Random House, Inc.

All trademarks are the property of their respective companies.

Book design by Chris Welch

Library of Congress Cataloging-in-Publication Data
Blackshaw, Pete.
Satisfied customers tell three friends, angry customers tell 3,000: running a business in today's consumer-driven world / Pete Blackshaw. — 1st ed.
p.   cm.
Includes index.
1. Consumer satisfaction. 2. Customer relations. 3. Organizational effectiveness.
I. Title.
HF5415.335.B55 2008
658.8'12—dc22
2007037908

ISBN: 978-0-385-52272-4

PRINTED IN THE UNITED STATES OF AMERICA

1   3   5   7   9   10   8   6   4   2

First Edition

DEDICATED TO MY FATHER,
WILLIAM J. BLACKSHAW,
AND TO JAMES HESKETT

CONTENTS

ACKNOWLEDGMENTS

There are so many individuals who have provided either assistance or inspiration to this project. First, my wife, Erika Brown, has been incredibly supportive and encouraging on so many levels, and I would certainly be remiss not to credit her for the original concept behind PlanetFeedback.com after we had a horrendous airline service experience. She's also the mother of my three beautiful children, Liam, Leila, and Sophia, a source of constant joy and daily inspiration.

My partners at Lark Productions, Lisa DiMona and Robin Dellabough, have patiently and thoughtfully worked with me on this project since its inception and are absolutely incredible. I also owe huge thanks to Talia Krohn and Roger Scholl of The Doubleday Publishing Group for their enthusiasm and help shaping the key theme and direction of the book. Thanks to others on the Doubleday team as well: Rachel Lapal, Meredith McGinnis, Nicole Dewey, and Rebecca Gardner.

Harvard Business School's James Heskett, for whom the

book is co-dedicated, inspired so much of the thinking in this book. His service-management course at HBS lit the spark of my obsession over the relationship between service and profitability, between listening and loyalty. Moreover, I will always be indebted to him for serving on the boards of PlanetFeedback and Intelliseek, and for always being available for trusted advice and counsel, especially during the tough periods.

The always inspirational Seth Godin deserves credit for the book title, and I'd be remiss not to also thank him for being a strong advocate with the venture community when I started my first company out of P&G. Greg Brummer has been invaluable with case studies, consumer interviews, surveys, all-around consumer smarts, and more. Karen Watts played a deeply appreciated early role in getting this project off the ground.

David Dintenfass, friend and P&G Associate Marketing Director, relentlessly pushed me to pursue this project, in particular helping me to think through the "Six Drivers of Credibility" framework. Other special sources of inspiration include Max Kalehoff and Sue MacDonald, Kelly Mooney, Ted McConnell, Greg Icenhower, Len Ellis, Jay Gooch, Raymond Buse, Laurent Flores, Chris Lansing, Doyle Estevick, Mark Marsan, Dave Evans, Tom Watson, Jeffrey Rayport, Tim Heath, Jon Sviokla, Jan Marie Zwiren, and my brother John Blackshaw. Denis Beausejour, friend, mentor, and former Global VP of Advertising at P&G, deserves credit for drilling into my head that at the end of the day, it's all about the consumer—always! The same goes for Robert Wehling, John Pepper, Vivienne Bechtold, Ted Woehrle, and Charlotte Otto. Former Grey Interactive leaders Norm Lehoullier and Orin Wechsberg have provided trusted advice and guidance.

Beth Thomas-Kim, Global Head of Consumer Services at Nestle, and Chairwoman of the Society of Consumer Affairs Professionals, provided thoughtful input and feedback, and no shortage of motivation, as did Tom Asher, Head of Consumer Affairs at Levi's. Bruce Ertmann, Toyota's Director of Consumer-Generated Media, has been a tremendous inspiration and help to me, especially on the "Defensive Branding Themes." Fred Siff of the University of Cincinnati was one of my very first customers, and his breakthrough work with new technologies continues to awe me. Scott Wilder of Intuit opened up an entirely new perspective on the power of online communities.

In my real job I draw invaluable perspective from so many current and former colleagues: Mike Nazzaro, Jay Stockwell, Betsy Cohen, Becky Hudepohl, Brian Schlessinger, Dan Mechem, Bill Stephenson, Jay Rampuria, Karen Watson, Doug Widmann, Andrew Ferrigno, Jim Savage, Jonathan Carson, Jerry Needel, Kate Niederhoffer, Amy Hatton, Alison Kalis, Lydia Worthington, Jenifer Putalavage, Charlie Buchwalter, Ori Levy, and Manish Bhatia. Mahendra Vora, Sundar Kadayam, Karthik Iyer, Chris Connaughton, Jonathan Schlerer, Matt Hurst, Mark Reed, and Natalie Glance all introduced (and humbled) me to the power and potential of advanced text analytics and unstructured data analysis. Oliver Fisher,

Mike Kunz, Jon Mamela, and Louis Goldner were part of the "alpha" group exploring the power of complaints. And interns Chandler Koglmeier and Chris McConnell introduced me to an entirely new level of understanding about social media.

Other key supporters and investors, now and in the past, include: Jack and Peg Wyant, Bill Hildebolt, Itzhak Fisher, Rick Kieser, John Gardner, Nick Nicholas, Fred Wilson, Jerry Colonna, Rick Lerner, and Ted Dintersmith.

Others have encouraged me to test my themes and hypotheses; among them: Rebecca Lieb and Erin Brenner, my editors at ClickZ, current and former Ad Tech leaders Susan Bratton and Drew Ianni, and Jack Neff of *Advertising Age,* who has always been a great sounding board and an occasional much appreciated skeptic. And of course I'd be remiss not to mention former and current collleagues and current and former board members of the Word-of-Mouth Marketing Association, who walk the talk on so much of what this book is all about: Jim Nail, Ed Keller, Paul Rand, Dave Balter, Rick Murray, Jackie Huba, John Bell, Sam Decker, Leslie Ford, Idil Cakim, Jamie Tedford, Peter Waldheim, Gary Spangler, Andy Sernovitz, Laura Schuler, Julie Wittes Schlack.

I'd also be remiss not to thank State Senator Art Torres, a tireless advocate for California's Hispanic and immigrant community, who represented one of the most diverse districts in the nation—from Chinatown to East L.A.—for teaching me how to listen to less obvious (but ever important) signals in the marketplace. He also empowered me to test new feedback models in the California legislature.

And let's not forget my parents: Jay Blackshaw, for always keeping me grounded in consumer-centered values; and to my dad, Bill Blackshaw, who passed away last year after living a beautiful 83 years, for being so supportive and cultivating a deep appreciation of all that can be good in advertising.

Most important, to all the consumers online, from PlanetFeedback.com and YouTube.com to Facebook and the millions of bloggers out there. Yeah, I know, it sounds hokey, but I lean on you every day for inspiration.

Introduction

Dell Inc. learned a hard lesson in July 2005, when the high-profile blogger and mainstream media pundit Jeff Jarvis had an unhappy experience with a new laptop computer. Angered by Dell's feeble and ineffective attempts to help him with his problem, Jarvis decided to vent his frustration by taking the computer giant to task on his blog, BuzzMachine.com. Jarvis used his "bloggy pulpit" to write an open letter to Dell's founder, Michael Dell, challenging the quality of the company's products and customer service, and assaulting its basic value proposition.

Soon, Jarvis's blog was inundated with Dell horror stories from other dissatisfied customers nationwide. BuzzMachine became one of the most visited sites on the Internet for several days, and a magnifier effect quickly kicked in, triggering yet another avalanche of letters voicing woe and outrage about the brand. Consumers then flocked to the company's Web site, posting vitriolic comments on its own message boards. By the time this flurry of communication reached critical mass, Jarvis's blog, and a host of newly created anti-Dell Web pages, were at the top of Google search results for "Dell."

Eventually, the Dell digital brouhaha grabbed the attention of mainstream media outlets, such as *PCWorld, Business-Week,* and *The Wall Street Journal.* Their reports not only generated more negative publicity but also encouraged more rounds of postings—a vicious circle, Internet-style. And in more bad news for Dell, these Web sites, blog postings, and message boards weren't like graffiti, which can be painted over or washed away. Instead, they left indelible digital tracks that would sustain negative impressions for excruciatingly long periods of time. (Just do an online search for "Dell sucks" today, more than two years after the Jarvis affair; www.ihatedell.net tops the list.)

Dell finally responded in late August 2005, announcing—in what was clearly a too-little, too-late effort at reconciliation—that it would respond to the comments on blogs. By then, of course, the damage was done. Dell, the pioneer in online selling, had been known for decades for its strong commitment to customization and individual treatment. But by late summer 2005, thanks to the work of a single blogger and the firestorm he caused, many people associated the brand with poor service and shoddy products.

The Jarvis issue virtually repeated itself in late 2007, when longtime prominent advertising critic Bob Garfield, frustrated with what he experienced as poor, unresponsive service by Comcast cable, launched a vicious anti-Comcast blog, ComcastMustDie.com, which almost immediately attracted over 700 overwhelmingly supportive comments. On the home page of his blog, Garfield wrote, "Congratulations. You are no longer just an angry, mistreated customer. Nor, I hope, are you just part of an e-mob. But you are a revolutionary, wresting control from the oligarchs, and claiming it for the consumer. Your power is enormous. Use it wisely."

For thousands of years, humankind has been telling its own story. Today, we're telling that story though an incessant, uninterrupted flurry of computer keystrokes. The global, multichannel exchange of information and ideas via the Internet is destined to become the Great Library of the modern age. Now that people are plugged in, they are rarely disconnected—and the result is a constant channel of thoughts and opinions from the brain directly to the screen. This is the era of what I call consumer-generated media, or CGM. What exactly is CGM? It is the currency of a new commercial relationship between business and consumers. It is the endless stream of comments, opinions, emotions, and personal stories about any and every company, product, service, or brand, which consumers can now post online and broadcast to millions of other consumers with the click of the mouse. It is the never-ending consumer-to-consumer conversation—across blogs, wikis, message boards, video-sharing sites, social networking pages, and more—about all the issues, topics, and experiences that matter to consumers themselves.

Throughout the history of commerce, consumers have been at the mercy of business. Consumers have traditionally had little information, limited access to one another, and few outlets for feedback and communication. But the Internet has changed all that. It's given consumers not only a collective voice but also a platform and a forum for those voices. Armed with a new suite of tools, resources, and technologies, consumers are no longer passive observers in the marketplace of ideas and commerce; they are actually defining and shaping the business landscape and the marketplace of tomorrow.

The Internet, specifically the now ubiquitous open-source, participatory Internet dubbed "Web 2.0," allows consumers, united by one common activity—purchasing goods and services from companies—to come together in an extended community. And increasingly, these consumers are united by a common frustration—a growing distrust of marketing and advertising. Consumer-generated media allows them to voice this distrust and to share their ideas, opinions, and emotions about every conceivable aspect of their consumer experiences—from how well a certain detergent removes stains to how upset they are about an outgoing CEO's compensation package.

Consumer-generated media is here to stay. Because what companies say to consumers about their products and services through their marketing and advertising channels is rapidly losing ground to what consumers say about those products and services to one another through their network of Internet-enabled channels. In today's online world, CGM is the true barometer of corporate and brand credibility. And as a result, the success of a company or brand rests on its ability to create and maintain credibility with its increasingly vocal consumers and customers on every front. Just ask Dell.

Or ask AOL. In June 2006, when Vincent Ferrari called to cancel his account, he went head-to-head with a combative service rep. Despite Ferrari's unambiguous, unequivocal, and repeated requests to cancel his account, the representative refused, persistently badgering Ferrari in a clear and infuriating effort to steer him toward maintaining the account (at one point the rep even asked to speak with Ferrari's father). As Ferrari grew more frustrated, the rep became increasingly rude and aggressive.

So what did Ferrari do? He recorded the twenty-one-minute conversation and posted the audio file first on his own blog, then on YouTube, where it received 62,827 views in two days. It was quickly picked up by the firebrand Consumerist .com blog, where it was described as "The Best Thing We Have Ever Posted." Matters only got worse for AOL soon afterward. Other subscribers began flooding the blogosphere with their own bad customer service experiences, and as it had with Dell, this deluge got the attention of mainstream media. The story was soon covered by CNBC and *The New York Times,* and Ferrari even appeared on the *Today* show. It was a public relations disaster for AOL, all thanks to a single customer call.

But Vincent Ferrari didn't create AOL's problems, and Jeff Jarvis didn't create Dell's, either. Their complaints simply exposed and magnified the problems that already existed. It wasn't just bad luck that both Jarvis and Ferrari had well-trafficked blogs, and that they both decided to blog about their bad experiences. In reality, it was the companies' lack of credibility that was responsible for the backlash Jarvis and Ferrari ignited. What did AOL and Dell in was the fact that they hadn't fostered open, trusting relationships with their customers; they simply weren't credible—and they were summarily punished for it.

The notion of credibility in business, marketing, and advertising has always intrigued me. Do companies tell the whole truth? Do they deceive consumers when they don't live up to the promise of their brand message? What is the relationship between credibility and business success?

In 1999, I left an amazing job at Procter & Gamble to put those questions to the ultimate test. I started PlanetFeedback, a consumer feedback Web site inspired in part by a group letter-writing exercise in the extremely popular Service Management course at Harvard Business School, which aggregated hundreds of thousands of consumers' letters, comments, and testimonials about brand experiences. I wasn't hired by any company, and I had no agenda (well . . . I *did* have a plan to make money off the data) other than to listen to and learn from consumers—I was like the Switzerland of consumer feedback. PlanetFeedback collected hundreds of highly engaged consumers' responses on thousands of issues and circumstances, and used these responses to crank out scorecards for companies based on measures of consumer loyalty, satisfaction, confidence, and trust. And what those scorecards told us was fascinating. They told us that successful brands, like Lands' End and Southwest Airlines, received off-the-charts high marks with consumers, while struggling brands, like Cingular (now AT&T) and Northwest Airlines, received painfully bad marks. (It is interesting that the now notorious MCI WorldCom boasted the lowest score across the entire site nearly a year before it came under media scrutiny for its accounting practices.) In other words, the scorecards told us that the most successful companies and brands were those perceived as most credible, and vice versa.

For Dell, the writing was on the wall long before Jeff Jarvis blasted his horn. A six-month analysis of customer letters by PlanetFeedback in 2003 showed that consumers considered Dell's customer service far worse than that of other large personal-computer manufacturers. Dell didn't offer customers the chance to inspect its products or talk to a manager in person, and its credibility problems included poor technical support and a reputation for unresponsive customer service. As one Dell customer told PlanetFeedback, "So, I have researched more about their customer service and am now scared to continue with this purchase." If Dell had addressed its credibility crisis by listening to its consumers and doing something about what they were saying, it could have prevented the 2005 nightmare. Instead, a swarm of digital termites ended up eating away at the reputation Dell had spent countless millions of dollars to create.

After I started PlanetFeedback, I learned very quickly that a consumer's willingness to engage or express himself or herself about a brand and that brand's perceived credibility are inextricably linked. After all, a brand, at heart, is a promise, and the brand's success is a measure of how well that promise is consistently met. In fact, some of the most viral—and hence most damaging—letters we saw at PlanetFeedback spoke of the gap between the brand promise (e.g., "We're here to serve you") and brand reality (e.g., never answering the 800 number). I also learned that there are specific trigger issues—such as billing or employee behavior or rebate policies—that either win the hearts of consumers or spark their outrage.

As the co-leader of the first interactive marketing team at Procter & Gamble, I had learned early on that the Web is a vast wellspring of information about consumer opinion and feedback. By leading over one hundred "test and learn" executions across every aspect of interactive marketing—from Web sites through online sampling to targeted Web ads—I had discovered that the Web is one giant listening platform, infinitely revealing of brand value. More valuable to companies than a hundred focus groups, the raw, unsolicited conversations on the Web not only reflect what consumers really think but also provide companies the opportunity to participate in the dialogue. The truth is that, on the Web, consumers have far greater power to broadcast their voices more loudly, more widely, and more efficiently than through even the best offline social networks. This, I soon found, can create both opportunities and headaches for companies.

By the time I left Procter & Gamble to start PlanetFeedback, three things had become clear. First, the consumer is the new center of the universe. Second, influential consumers have a whole new level of power and influence that puts new pressure on brands to be genuinely credible and to carry through on their brand promises on every level. Third, in order to maintain this credibility, businesses have no choice but to listen obsessively to consumers on their terms. That was the new reality.

Armed with that insight, I raised over $30 million in venture funding to start PlanetFeedback. A couple years later, we merged with Intelliseek, a search-based technology firm that was beginning to focus on making sense of millions of consumer conversations on Internet message boards. By combining our cash, client rosters, and management teams, we were well positioned to begin carving out a fresh new niche around consumer-generated media, the term I coined to describe all the online media—including blogs, video- and photo-sharing sites, social networking pages, online forums, message boards, and product review sites—through which consumers can convey their opinions to one another. After we had worked with clients such as Toyota, BMW, Sony, Sprint, and Time Warner on over one hundred projects, the Nielsen Company acquired us and rolled us up with our top competitors, BuzzMetrics and Trendum, to create a new entity now known as Nielsen Online.

Our expanded lens into the mind of the consumer has provided me with a fascinating view of both the opportunities and the challenges facing major brands and corporations. Just think about it—with tens of millions of conversations, a significant percentage of which implicate companies or brands, being cranked out on a daily basis, the Internet becomes what amounts to a massive real-time accountability scorecard for today's businesses. And this "digital accountability trail" is essentially a barometer of good, bad, or outright stupid business decisions.

The revolution in Internet technologies has added an entirely new dimension to companies' credibility. As we saw with Jeff Jarvis and Vincent Ferrari, the new forms of online media—from blogs to wikis to YouTube to MySpace—provide anyone and everyone with the tools to communicate a wide swath of consumer experiences to the masses. Consumers have always had plenty to say about companies; in the pre-Web days, they simply opted not to express themselves because it was much more difficult, and time consuming, to share their message with a large audience. Now, speaking out is nearly as easy as breathing, and that fact is changing the rules for businesses around the globe.

But there is some good news. The Web not only provides consumers with a platform for expressing their preferences, grievances, and experiences but also provides companies with a means of listening to them. It gives you and your competitors the invaluable opportunity to tune in to the issues and buzz surrounding your company or product. That's the thing about this new age of transparency: the information is out there for *everyone*—not just marketers and advertisers but also managers, product developers, Web site designers, and executives at all levels of the organization—to gather and interpret. Use it to your advantage, or ignore it at your peril.

The reality of our online world has turned credibility into the most important asset for today's companies. This book is about how to build and grow that asset, using the techniques and strategies I've learned through years of helping companies interpret, analyze, and respond to the messages of today's vocal consumer.

But before you go on, I implore you to read, reread, and commit to these three truths, truths that inform this entire book. They are

1. Businesses no longer hold absolute sway over the decisions and behavior of consumers.

2. The longer companies refuse to accept the influence of consumer-to-consumer communication and perpetuate the old ways of doing business, the more they will alienate and drive away their customers.

3. To succeed in a world where consumers now control the conversation, and where satisfied customers tell three friends while angry customers tell 3,000, companies absolutely must achieve *credibility on every front.*

Chapter 1

The Credibility of the Commons and the Core Credibility Drivers

n his famous treatise "The Tragedy of the Commons," Garrett Hardin demonstrates the fundamental conflict between individual interests and the common good. Hardin describes how, when a plot of land is commonly available to all the farmers in a village, one farmer after another brings his livestock to graze, blind to the inevitable consequence of depleting the land through overgrazing. Writes Hardin:

> Adding together the component partial utilities, the rational herdsman concludes that the only sensible course for him to pursue is to add another animal to his herd. And another. . . . But this is the conclusion reached by each and every rational herdsman sharing a commons. Therein is the tragedy. Each man is locked into a system that compels him to increase his herd without limit—in a world that is limited.

In the twenty-first century, consumers' attention, and trust, is like that commons—a limited resource that is easily depleted. In today's world of high-speed broadband and commercial-free TiVo, consumers have less attention and patience for advertising and marketing than ever before. Ad saturation, deceptive messaging, and mismanaged expectations contribute to consumers' dwindling trust in companies.

So businesses must work even harder to maintain market share, reinforce brand messages, and communicate new ideas, in order to preserve their competitive advantage—in other words, get more use out of the commons than the other farmers. But when businesses simply spend ad dollars to buy awareness without developing strategies to cultivate credibility and earn trust, they will run into trouble. For there no longer exists a top-down relationship between businesses and consumers; while marketers used to have control over the message and could count on the masses to follow along whether they liked it or not, today, the consumer is the boss. In a speech given in October 2006, Charlotte Otto, global external relations officer for Procter & Gamble, said we are delusional if we think that, as communications practitioners, we can "control" the message or "manage the medium." "Now more than ever," she said, "consumers own our brands. Consumers own our messages. Consumers own the conversation about how, where, and if they invite our brands into their lives."

Which brings us back to credibility. Credibility may not be on your balance sheet, but it's the best asset you've got. Credibility is the only valid currency in this vast and noisy marketplace. So what exactly constitutes credibility, and how do you learn how to harness it?

Credibility in today's marketing environment is the product of six core drivers. Most of them are interrelated, but they require different strategies and tactics to fully realize. These critical credibility drivers are

1. Trust
2. Authenticity
3. Transparency
4. Listening
5. Responsiveness
6. Affirmation

1. TRUST

Trust is perhaps the most critical driver of credibility. Trust implies confidence, dependability, and faith in a company or product. It is achieved through honest, ethical, straightforward, consistent, and predictable business practices. Unfortunately, trust is a diminishing resource for today's businesses. As a 2004 study by Intelliseek and Forrester Research found, consumers trust other consumers far more than they trust companies or brands, and they consistently distrust marketing techniques used by brands. This finding was recently reaffirmed in a 2007 Nielsen global trust study. Virtually every global region lined up similarly.

Trust is the credibility driver that is most closely linked to performance. After all, who is going to trust a product or service that doesn't perform as promised? Remember, a brand is a promise, and consumers assess brands by the extent to which they live up to that promise. Trust also includes an element of predictability. Consumers tend not to like nasty surprises. Ask yourself: Do your company's ad campaigns stretch the truth? Do your claims match what the product can actually do or deliver? Does your product or service consistently and predictably perform as promised? Companies that nurture trust with consumers can honestly answer yes to these questions.

But this isn't always enough. It's important for companies to adhere to a policy of honest, straightforward communication on the Web as well. Companies with high levels of trust don't create blogs pretending to be written by consumers, they don't "seed" message boards with positive comments supposedly from consumers, and they always present truthful and useful information on their Web sites. As multiple studies conducted by Nielsen showed, brand Web sites are the second most "trusted" communications vehicles after word of mouth. And intuitively this makes sense: After all, Web sites are there to help consumers find information and solve problems.

Here are five examples of how companies have established and maintained high levels of trust among their customers.

Lands' End has built a name for itself by nurturing a trust-based relationship with consumers. The mail-order house's clothing and apparel consistently measure up to its claims, and the company is exceptionally responsive if consumers question that trust. It makes a sincere effort to manage every consumer response and to replace any unsatisfactory product. The Lands' End product guarantee is unconditional. It reads: "If you're not satisfied with any item, simply return it to us at any time for an exchange or refund of its purchase price. We mean every word of it. Whatever. Whenever. Always. But to make sure this is perfectly clear, we've decided to simplify it further. GUARANTEED. PERIOD." The Lands' End call center is attentive to all calls, and customer service is considered the highest priority. The company has 24/7 toll-free lines, and each of the 200,000 e-mails it receives annually gets a personal response. Lands' End Live even lets consumers talk or "chat" online directly with Lands' End call support folks while shopping at Landsend.com. Consumers trust that Lands' End's products and customer service will always meet or exceed their expectations, and the net result is extraordinary high levels of loyalty and an off-the-charts digital trail of positive consumer-generated media.

Johnson & Johnson is another trusted company, with a hundred-year tradition of open, transparent communication, even in times of crisis. Johnson & Johnson produces thousands of branded health-care products, including toiletries, baby products, pharmaceuticals, and medical diagnostic equipment. Can you even compete in these categories without a heavy dose of trust in the equation? The former CEO James Burke's honest and sincere handling of the

Tylenol tampering crisis in the early 1980s is legendary. The brand not only showed genuine compassion for the people who got sick from taking the tainted drugs but also took extraordinary steps to rebuild consumers' trust and confidence. When the brand was put back on store shelves, Johnson & Johnson changed its packaging to include three layers of tamper protection, two more than recommended by the Food and Drug Administration.

Canon USA, maker of a range of electronics products, from camcorders to digital cameras, has set a higher bar for trust in a product category marred by high levels of frustration and distrust. While Canon's customer service operation suffers from many of the same troubles as the electronics industry as a whole, the company is building credibility through its commitment to quality and innovation. Canon spends approximately 10 percent of its net sales on research and development each year, nearly twice the percentage of its key competitors. High-quality products nurture trust, which is expressed by a preponderance of positive online ratings and reviews, as well as high levels of consumer loyalty and repeat purchase. Consumers respond favorably to the Canon sales force, one of the most skilled in the industry, and this too makes for fantastic CGM. As a result, Canon consistently outperforms other major electronics brands, was named among the most admired companies by *Fortune* magazine, and ranked number 25 of one hundred top brands by *BusinessWeek* magazine.

Southwest Airlines consistently tops the CGM charts on PlanetFeedback.com and receives consistent positive online buzz. This airline cultivates trust by carefully managing consumer expectations and making each and every business decision on the basis of its single product claim: low prices. In fact, when an employee suggested the airline might offer a light in-flight meal on the Houston to Las Vegas flight, founder and then CEO Herb Kelleher shot it down immediately because it would have driven up ticket prices. But consumers don't mind bringing their own snacks on a Southwest flight. Why? Because when they fly Southwest, they don't expect a luxury experience; instead, they trust they are getting exactly what Southwest promises: the lowest ticket prices, period. This credibility has gone a long way to generate positive CGM for the company and is one of the reasons why Southwest is one of the few airlines in the business to actually turn a profit.

Mazda, on the other hand, is still reeling from the hit its credibility took when it was discovered that the "consumer blog" the company created was in fact a stealth effort by its advertising agency. Bloggers identified the deception immediately and tarred and feathered Mazda for the breach of trust. And because a digital trail is indelible, the backlash follows the automaker to this day; if you search "Mazda blog" on Google, all you will see is hostility. Mazda violated the trust principle and is still paying the price.

2. AUTHENTICITY

A company that projects authenticity is one that is perceived to be real and sincere, consistent and genuine. Trust and authenticity, of course, are inextricably linked—consumers trust brands that come across as real and sincere. Authenticity is an especially important driver of credibility in the digital age, when consumers have more tools at their disposal to prove or disprove the claims a company makes. In a time when detailed information about companies' products, business practices, and histories is readily available, there is a much higher premium on authenticity.

Authenticity is becoming increasingly important as consumers grow more and more cynical about advertising and brands. Now, even the most trusting consumers ask: Is the company real and sincere? Does it speak with a genuine voice or one that is phony and contrived? Are its motivations pure or manipulative? Does the company *truly* care about me?

There are important nuances that affect perceptions of a company's authenticity. We're entering a new era of marketing, in which consumers are evaluating brands based on a much more stringent set of criteria, bringing their own values—and even causes—to the table. Here are three examples of ways companies have boosted their authenticity by appealing to the values of their core customers.

Chick-fil-A, a fast-food restaurant chain, has earned an enviable mantle of credibility by doing things in an authentic way. At the root of its business is faith and unabashed belief in serving the Lord, and this principle guides how the company does business and serves its customers. All Chick-fil-A restaurants are closed on Sundays so that employees can spend the day in worship; unit managers are expected to contribute to the well-being of their community and their employees through servant leadership—leadership that focuses not so much on what I want as on how to help others get what they want. And as a result, despite being open only six days each week, Chick-fil-A has the highest annual average unit volume of any fast-food chicken restaurant in the nation. In fact, its unit sales compare favorably with those of McDonald's, Burger King, and Wendy's despite fifty-two fewer selling days per year.

Northern California's Peet's coffee has seen remarkable growth in the past few years, primarily because it is viewed as a less corporate and more authentic brand than Starbucks. The Peet's brand appeals to the most fervent coffee lovers because it is sincere and genuine in its commitment to quality. I visited Peet's last year and witnessed the attention the company puts into every bag of coffee beans. The work is not outsourced; most of the testing takes place right at corporate headquarters in Emeryville, California. Inspectors diligently taste every batch of beans with the intensity of fine vintners. But Peet's authenticity goes beyond just picking and inspecting beans; the company employs a unique artisan roasting method. As its Web site states, "Developing these roasting skills takes time. . . . We require each of our roasters to make a ten-year employment commitment. A roaster is deemed to have enough experience to have truly mastered the craft only after three to four years of training. We roast by hand, not by computer. We roast in small batches, paying close attention to the individual characteristics that each coffee or blend requires. We roast all thirty-two of our coffees every day. And we roast to taste, not to color."

To ensure its integrity, the company deliberately has not grown as fast as Starbucks; it views franchising as a potential compromise of quality and service. This approach has helped Peet's maintain a high level of authenticity among consumers.

Ben & Jerry's (now owned by Unilever) has built a loyal customer base by being authentic about its commitment to giving back to the community. In 1985, the company used profits to establish the Ben & Jerry's Foundation, which at one point donated over $1.1 million each year to environmental and social causes and distributes grants to community-based action groups in the state of Vermont. Ben & Jerry's also takes stands on various social issues (such as fuel efficiency, peace advocacy, and support for small-scale family farms) on its Web site, and the company upholds its strong commitment to social justice and the environment in everything that it does. This authenticity resonates strongly with consumers who buy Ben & Jerry's ice cream because they view it as some sort of bridge between earth and man. It also helps that the company Web site maintains the down-to-earth vibe and folksy sense of humor that pervade the company's products—after all, it's hard not to like a company that lets consumers design their own flavors and names ice cream after rock musicians.

In a perfect example of why you don't mess with authenticity, when Ben & Jerry's once tried to bring in a "professional" CEO to drive further growth, the move backfired, alarming both faithful customers and its own executive ranks. After a year, the experiment was declared a failure and the CEO was fired.

3. TRANSPARENCY

Today, through search engines such as Google and other popular research tools, such as Wikipedia, consumers can learn all there is to know about your company—not just about the external product but also about what goes into making it, such as product ingredients, business policies, executive compensation, and labor practices. Most Wikipedia entries for major corporations—such as McDonald's, Nike, P&G, Frito-Lay, and Coca-Cola—make it easy not only to find official statistics and facts about the corporation but also to link directly to third-party blogs, customer commentary, or other revealing documents. The Internet simply creates more exposure for companies and brands. So to win credibility and build consumers' trust, companies must be 100 percent transparent in everything they do.

Transparent corporations are open about their practices and policies, and make their most relevant facts and data widely known (without releasing legally privileged information). Transparency involves openness and visibility, and it's increasingly important in the age of CGM.

In many cases, improving transparency may be as simple as enlarging the fine print of product information or making labels more clear and easy to read. In other cases, transparency involves willingly making disclosures in advertising or packaging. Pharmaceutical companies, which are required by law to disclose risks and side effects, practice what we might call forced transparency. But disclosing the bare minimum required by law is often not enough to achieve true transparency. What's more, the *way* in which the company chooses to relay these disclosures can affect its credibility—if the announcer in a television commercial for a drug reads the list of negative side effects slowly and clearly at the start of the commercial, for example, the product will be perceived as more transparent than if he runs through the list at warp speed during the last five seconds.

In today's online world, activist groups are getting increasingly good at finding—and broadcasting—skeletons in companies' closets. Such groups, which thanks to ease of joining via the Internet, have more members and wield more influence than ever before, are putting even greater pressure on companies to be more transparent by using multimedia forms of CGM to further their agendas. The animal rights group PETA, for example, has made very effective use of online video to raise awareness. It employs undercover investigators to secretly film corporate mistreatment of animals and then posts those videos on its Web site; when PETA posted video footage of England-based KFC contractors dropkicking chickens like soccer balls before slaughtering them, public outrage erupted, and Yum! Brands, parent of KFC was immediately forced to acknowledge the existence of such practices and deal with them in a more transparent manner. So the corporation launched an animal responsibility program that included supplier audits as well as a social responsibility program that made information about how KFC interacts with its customers and suppliers available to the public.

And with globalization and free trade spiking sensitivities about labor conditions in other countries, labor activist groups, too, have become increasingly vocal in creating CGM. Web sites such as BuyBlue.org rate companies not just on the price and value of their products but also on their political donations and their practices relating to the environment, labor, human rights, and corporate and social responsibility. WakeUp Wal-Mart, a campaign that is union funded and organized, not only broadcasts the low-cost retailer's every misstep online in living color but also galvanizes supporters for tiny localized campaigns and offers current and former disgruntled employees the chance to tell their stories through online forums. In recent years, groups like this one have forced Wal-Mart to be more transparent about its hiring practices, wage and benefits standards, and environmental policies.

There are also countless blogs that take corporations to task on key labor and sustainability issues by posting incriminating information and encouraging consumers to boycott offending companies. These blogs link to a host of like-minded sites that also point out the transgressions of various companies in bright, living pixels, creating a classic magnifier effect. Bloggers' campaigns against specific companies may involve e-mail blasts, snail-mail blasts, and letters to government agencies. The more aggressive sites even encourage readers to visit the company's physical locations and make their views known there. While many of these tactics are extreme, perhaps even bordering on illegal, they clearly illustrate how effective CGM can be in galvanizing huge numbers of people from all over the world to speak out against a company or corporation.

So to avoid the wrath of such vocal activists, businesses have no choice but to be completely open and honest about their ethical stances. Patagonia, which produces outdoor clothing and casual footwear, for example, notes on its Web site:

> Our definition of quality includes a mandate for building products and working with processes that cause the least harm to the environment. We evaluate raw materials, invest in innovative technologies, rigorously police our waste and use a portion of our sales to support groups working to make a real difference.

By being so forthcoming—in other words, transparent—about all dimensions of its commitment to a sustainable environment, Patagonia has earned credibility with everyone from "green" activist bloggers to regular shoppers who care about the environment.

The lesson for any business, from a fast-food chain to a

clothing manufacturer and beyond: Be transparent about your company or product. Today, companies can either let others tell their stories—which brings the risk of miscommunication, exaggeration, or even manipulation—or they can preempt or at least neutralize such moves by explaining the facts themselves. It's not in the interest of any company to hide information; activist groups and others, including everyday consumers, will just uncover it, then spread it with their own spin. There will be a lot more damage to your reputation, and your credibility, if consumers find out the information you're trying to hide from a catchy YouTube video.

4. LISTENING

In an article for *Ad Age,* the outspoken Comcast critic Bob Garfield suggests that the art of listening is a big missing piece in the marketing equation. And he is absolutely right; listening is a critical component of doing business, in every field or industry. A company that truly listens is one that is approachable, invites open conversation, encourages feedback, and embraces "360° listening," which involves absorbing input from all directions—whether internal, external, CGM, or beyond.

This is a big issue today, because the more consumers are in control, the more they want to feel respected and valued. Even a simple signal—such as providing the URL of the company feedback form in all advertising materials, at the point of purchase, and on all packaging—that a company is open for conversation can improve the relationship. In addition, companies can create specific e-mail addresses that encourage consumers to give feedback. For instance, in 2007, Home Depot set up wearelistening@homedepot.com as a way of encouraging unhappy consumers to contact the company and set up a task force dedicated to addressing every issue raised. As CEO Frank Blake wrote, "We're committed to being the company that helped set the standard for customer service excellence in home improvement. Please continue to hold us accountable. You have my personal assurance that every effort will be made to address your concerns." This commitment was a major step toward winning back customers who were disenchanted with Home Depot's customer service. Home Depot learned that half the game in earning respect and credibility with consumers is simply listening, and showing that you care.

Listening drives credibility in several important ways. First, the process of gathering open, honest feedback humanizes the company, forcing it to step off its corporate pedestal and truly connect with consumers on their level.

Second, listening drives credibility because it forms the foundation of relationship and loyalty building. Virtually everyone has an emotional desire to be heard, and a company that fulfills that need will have a huge leg up over competitors who ignore it. A 2003 Forrester study suggested that consumers are far more favorable to brands that have a friendly welcome mat, or show an interest in hearing what their consumers have to say. Encouraging feedback via Web sites, blogs, and other forms of CGM is a good way to open channels of communication and position your company as a proactive listener.

Third, the process of listening shapes the external conversation. When consumers think companies are not listening, they will go to other outlets for expression. And while you can monitor the content and flow of feedback on your company's Web site, once consumers post elsewhere, you relinquish this control. In fact, a big reason consumers spread CGM all over the Internet is that they don't feel they are being heard.

Companies should also extend their listening platforms to hugely popular Web sites such as YouTube and Facebook. Today, because anyone can set up a profile on the social networking sites—for free—in minutes, many companies are setting up pages and encouraging customers to "friend them," or join their networks. This practice lowers the barrier to open conversation and feedback while heightening awareness about the company's brand or product among a highly engaged audience.

Companies can find good examples of how to use CGM to foster listening in the 2008 presidential campaigns. Candidates ranging from Hillary Clinton to John McCain have all set up pages on social networking sites. MySpace in particular has become a de facto campaign organizing platform. The "friends list" is today's equivalent of the old paper sign-up sheet; and because clicking "subscribe" or "add friend" is so much easier than taking a trip to your local campaign headquarters, the major candidates have longer lists of "friends" than ever before. Further, because comment boxes provide supporters—and detractors—direct lines to the candidates (or at least their staff), social networking pages are a great way of tuning in to—and even participating in—conversations among voters about the issues that matter to them the most. This is equally true for companies.

Here are four ways that successful corporations are fostering credibility through listening.

Toyota Motor Corporation, one of our top clients at Nielsen Online for over four years, has learned to listen to online discussion very attentively. Dozens of Toyota engineers now review CGM data related to quality—whether on blogs, boards, forums, or auto-enthusiasts' Web sites—on a daily basis. Bill Stephenson, the auto industry executive who spearheaded our relationship with Toyota, noted that "we're seeing a fundamentally new mind-set among leading auto manufacturers around listening. Every voice counts." Given that there are over 100 million blogs in the U.S. alone (my estimate by publication time), Toyota has learned that the net output of feedback far exceeds what a company could receive through standard surveys. And as a result, Toyota has gained invaluable suggestions for how to improve its products.

Similarly, Bank of America has developed a powerful new model of "360" listening that incorporates all forms of consumer data—not just feedback sent directly to the company but also unsolicited conversations in multiple CGM venues. Bank of America not only conducts traditional research and reads and responds to letters, e-mails, and 800 calls but also listens to the broader and more diverse conversation taking place on blogs, wikis, Web sites, and message boards beyond its own "listening borders." Like Toyota, Bank of America views 360 listening as fundamental to its strategy and competitive advantage.

While many sellers of consumer packaged goods leave much to be desired on the customer feedback front, Unilever's Dove Skin-Care brand is setting an impressively high bar on listening. Do you have an opinion about the Dove brand or the "Real Women" campaign? Dove aggressively encourages feedback through online forums and communities available on its Web site. This accessibility has fed a broader perception that the brand is real, authentic, and in touch with the goals, aspirations, and feelings of women today.

McDonald's, by contrast, comes across as though the last thing it would ever want to do is listen to consumers. The "contact us" form on McDonald's Web site is not only painfully user-unfriendly but nearly impossible to find. For many consumers, especially the ones who post public complaints on the Web, such inaccessibility represents a big, credibility-eroding disconnect with the cheery "come on in" message McDonald's television advertising tries to convey.

5. RESPONSIVENESS

Responsiveness is how well a company addresses, reacts to, and manages consumer feedback. It's one thing for companies to be listeners, but if they don't respond to what they hear, they don't get full credit. Consumers today have been conditioned, through years of experience, to believe that companies will always try to put on a great face but in the end not go the distance to address their concerns. And this is partly why companies who defy consumers' low expectations gain such high marks in credibility. In conversations and focus groups with users of PlanetFeedback, we found that consumers were more motivated to offer feedback on a customer service Web site when the company had been unresponsive to them previously, but that when the company actually did respond to their comments or complaints, they were overjoyed.

Lenovo, the world's third largest PC maker, for example, rises above the low expectations customers tend to have of computer companies by actually reaching into the CGM space to address and respond to concerns. In fact, one of Lenovo's key executives frequently visits message boards to respond to issues personally. Consumers see such responsiveness as a sign of sincerity and genuine appreciation for their problems or suggestions.

In early 2006, Wal-Mart received a barrage of negative publicity when consumers searching on its Web site for DVDs with African American themes were recommended titles such as *The Planet of the Apes: The Complete TV Series, Charlie and the Chocolate Factory,* and *The Incredible Mr. Limpet.* The controversy began when a lone blogger named San Diego Johnny discovered the curious—and racist—software glitch. Soon, however, the story was picked up by other bloggers, and eventually the mainstream media, triggering widespread outrage and even boycotts.

But Wal-Mart managed to minimize the damage to its credibility by being responsive. As soon as the company was alerted to the embarrassing and offensive problem, it issued a sincere apology and shut down the entire cross-selling system until it was fixed. As a result, Wal-Mart was, for the most part, forgiven.

Sometimes, companies are faced with negative publicity stemming from false rumors. In these cases, it's just as important—maybe more so—for the companies to respond. For example, in April 2006, the popular firebrand blog Consumerist.com accused the California-based smoothie chain Jamba Juice of using milk in its nondairy smoothie. That was not, in fact, the case, but the posting was picked up by twenty other blogs and viewed a total of 23,000 times. Wisely, Jamba Juice traced the mistake to a customer service rep who had misspoken when talking to a blogger, then posted a statement to The Consumerist setting the record straight. Not everyone who saw the initial accusation saw the statement, but it was still successful in stopping the rumor in its tracks.[1]

RESPONDING TO TALK TRIGGERS

All product categories have what I term "talk triggers"—aspects of the brand experience that produce disproportionate amounts of comments and conversation online. Companies need to listen and be especially responsive to CGM surrounding these areas.

For example, in 2006, a consumer posted a letter to PlanetFeedback complaining about his new, defective large-screen TV. The TV was under warranty, but Best Buy was unresponsive to his requests to replace it. What infuriated him the most, however, was that it just so happened that he was having a Super Bowl party at the end of the week. A major event such as the Super Bowl is a common talk trigger, so his letter to PlanetFeedback had a viral effect, generating over one hundred responses from other consumers, mostly sympathetic. Eventually Best Buy apologized and replaced the TV, but it was too little too late; hundreds of consumers now thought of the company as a chain with shoddy products that doesn't respond to complaints.

Holiday shopping is another talk trigger. Consumers love to share recommendations, suggestions, and online word of mouth about the gifts they are planning to buy or hoping to receive. Companies would do well to be especially vigilant in listening to CGM before and during the holidays to see what kinds of products are generating the most buzz. Companies would also do well to pay attention to these conversations right after the holidays, when people are talking about what they did or didn't like about the gifts they bought or received.

Some talk triggers are general; others are more industry-specific. Billing is a major talk trigger in the wireless industry, as are technical support for the computer sector and safety for the automotive industry. In the fast-food business, issues related to hygiene are disproportionately viral. This is one reason why Yum! Brands, the parent company of KFC and Taco Bell, faced such major backlash in February 2007, when a video showing dozens of rats scampering through a New York City KFC/Taco Bell restaurant was posted to the Web. Almost immediately, the footage was picked up by all the major TV networks, all of whom ran it on that evening's news, and the story was reported for days in newspapers around the country. Yet even as this massive scandal forced a shutdown of the Greenwich Village location and prompted a surge of health inspections that resulted in the closure of over ninety other restaurants throughout the city, many consumers noted online that Yum! did not respond quickly enough.

Companies need to listen to CGM surrounding talk triggers and to develop marketing strategies that amplify the good news and respond to the bad. This is why car manufacturers with strong safety records stress safety in commercials, and it is why many electronics retailers with reputations for bad customer service are starting to implement more consumer-friendly return or repair policies. Smart companies know what consumers value and talk about; the challenge is making sure to respond to the issues that are most important.

6. AFFIRMATION

Affirmation refers to a consensus of positive or negative "truths" about a business or a brand. Not surprisingly, CGM is the primary barometer of affirmation because truth, in the eyes of a growing number of consumers and buyers, is defined as the collective judgment of peers or consumers. Increasingly, consumers are relying on CGM or online word of mouth to reach conclusions about products, brands, corporations, and services. So, in order to be truly credible in today's digital world, the claims a company makes about itself or its products must be affirmed by the things consumers are saying to one another through message board comments, online reviews, blog posts, shared photos and videos, and so on.

Just consider the car-buying process. A buyer may see a TV ad claiming a particular car is highest in its class for safety, is roomier than its competitors, or has ecofriendly features. That buyer is likely to go straight to Google or Edmunds.com to confirm those claims. This is where the affirmation principle kicks into gear. If messages on the Edmunds site contradict the claims, warning perhaps of malfunctioning air bags or poor gas mileage, not only is that buyer unlikely to buy that particular model but he or she is unlikely to purchase any car by that manufacturer ever. Why? Because in that consumer's mind, the maker's credibility is shot.

This type of positive or negative affirmation is now informing most purchasing behavior. In fact, if you talk to an auto dealer today, he or she will tell you that typical car buyers almost always walk into the dealership with a stack of online reviews or comments about the cars they are looking at. This form of due diligence puts pressure on carmakers to deliver on the claims they make in their marketing and advertising, and it significantly elevates buyer power.

Pampers is an example of a credible brand that is constantly affirmed through CGM. The brand has always positioned itself as one that makes superior products, and this claim is consistently reinforced by comments from both experts and parents in online forums, communities, and blogs. In fact, if you search for "diapers" on Google, you'll find 1.5 million first-person comments about Pampers, most of which praise the brand for effectiveness, durability, absorbency, and overall value. Some comments are quite detailed and descriptive (perhaps too descriptive—after all, it *is* a diaper) about the product's most subtle nuances.

General Motors banked on the power of affirmation when it ran a campaign encouraging consumers to "Google Pontiac" as a show of confidence about its product. MediaPost wrote, "This GM spot was significant because it ended with an unusual call to action: 'Don't take our word for it. Google Pontiac and discover for yourself.' " Only companies that are already credible can get away with this; when consumers saw that Pontiac's search results did confirm all the positive things the company was saying about the car, its credibility ratings shot up even higher.

Home Depot, by contrast, is struggling for positive affirmation with its new Eco Options program. While the company stresses its commitment to selling products that meet the highest sustainability standards, many online conversations indicate otherwise; Home Depot has been criticized widely—and vocally—across the blogosphere for continuing to sell environmentally irresponsible products such as toxic pesticides and inefficient lightbulbs.

Countless other brands are also having their environmental, or "green," efforts either affirmed or not affirmed online. In fact, environmental claims draw some of the most skepticism—and online conversations—among socially conscious consumers. As a result, companies need to be extra careful to make sure they live up to their green promises.

There is one caveat to affirmation: It isn't always fair and rational. In some cases, the data informing a decision may not even be accurate. This, of course, is the Catch-22 of the CGM environment. Social media tools such as Wikipedia, a user-generated encyclopedia on which multiple authors create and edit definitions on an enormous range of topics, are often regarded as authoritative consensuses of opinion. But this "wisdom of the crowd," or collective judgment of anonymous Internet users, is not always right; a few misinformed or biased users can significantly sway consumer attitudes and in many cases damage the credibility of a business or brand. This is why it is even more important for companies to become part of the conversation by being transparent, listening and responding to feedback, and fostering trust and loyalty with their customers.

In his recent book *All Marketers Are Liars,* Seth Godin states that the most effective marketers tell the best—that is, the most convincing, the most relevant, or the most entertaining—stories about their brands. I would argue that today companies don't just need to tell good stories; they also need to tell *credible* ones. Credibility rules the day, and if a company's "story" doesn't foster trust, if it doesn't convey transparency and authenticity, if it isn't informed by listening and responding to customers, and it isn't positively affirmed by what consumers are saying to one another, then it's just another phony story. And consumers will see right through it.

In our digital age, consumers are not only changing the terms of the buyer-seller covenant but also redefining the marketplace and rewriting the rules for doing business. In the chapters that follow, I'll explain how you can build more credibility into your business by learning how to tap into, measure, and respond to the conversations going on among today's empowered consumers.

Chapter 2

The Consumer's the Boss: Today's New Consumer-Generated World

When I worked as a press secretary in the California legislature, we had a rule of thumb for reading and responding to constituent letters. For every letter we received, we assumed a hundred constituents felt the same way but didn't bother to write. So, naturally, we took each letter seriously. My boss, Senator Art Torres, represented what was arguably the nation's most diverse legislative district, encompassing East Los Angeles, downtown Los Angeles, Chinatown, Korea Town, and mostly white South Pasadena. He didn't have a choice; in order to understand what this complex population was talking about, he had to carefully tune in.

Although only a small percentage of the constituents ever made the effort to write, their letters were surprisingly representative of popular opinion. So they were a great barometer of the district's "pulse" on various topics, from school reform to economic development. Often the letters served as tip sheets telling us on which issues we should sponsor legislation, hold a constituent meeting, or orchestrate a media event. The letters also provided a good read on what we were doing wrong, and the strength of the opposition to our policies or priorities.

One question I constantly asked myself during those five years was: What if many more citizens were communicating directly to us? What if the barriers to providing feedback or speaking out were lowered? How would that change the game? Would it enhance the quality of conversation about issues? Might it lead to some fresh ideas and insights? Could it effect real and lasting change?

In 1993, while working with the senator's team on insurance reform, I began to glimpse the answer to those questions. California had just set up its own equivalent of C-SPAN called the California Channel, which broadcast live state government proceedings, floor debates, and hearings in Sacramento. As an experiment, we in the senator's office invited anyone watching a live televised hearing about insurance topics to call an 800 number during the hearing and provide feedback on the issue. It was the first real-time test of its kind anywhere in the country—we beat President Clinton's first "electronic town hall" meeting by about a month—and the results surprised everyone. During our very first hearing, we received nearly twenty calls, totaling an hour and a half of live testimonials on a range of concerns and firsthand experiences related to insurance. Before this, constituents would have had to travel hours and hours, at their own expense, to Sacramento to participate in the proceedings. But by creating this "interactive hearing," in which people could participate from their own homes, we enabled more people to share their opinions, which dramatically improved the quality, relevance, and breadth of this critically important conversation.

That insurance hearing was a huge epiphany. It proved that technology could play a vital role in transforming and strengthening the consumer feedback loop. We created a more meaningful conversation on insurance reform at a time when authentic debate was being muffled by a stagnant pool of special interests: lawyers, doctors, and insurance companies. By using new technology to lower the barrier to expression, we enabled constituents who would otherwise have felt inhibited, time constrained, or inconvenienced to step up to the plate.

This is not to suggest that real dialogue or meaningful conversation didn't exist before the latest technological advances—of course it did. Voters (and consumers) have always had important, influential things to say. But now, with all the digital tools of expression available, such conversation has become a million times easier. And the more adept people become in using the Internet as a social communications and networking medium, the more they are learning that their voices matter—that they no longer have to automatically place their trust, faith, and confidence in politicians, corporations, and special interests. And they are renegotiating their relationships with these groups based on a bold new set of operating covenants and conditions at a rapidly accelerating pace. My Sacramento experience feels as if it took place in the Stone Age compared with where things are today.

When I moved from the political arena to the business world, I soon discovered that the same dynamics of consumer opinion and expression I'd observed in politics applied to companies and brands. When one of my professors at Harvard Business School, Jim Heskett, introduced the notion that for every hundred consumers who had a complaint, only a small percentage would actually bother to say anything, I immediately saw that, when it came to feedback, consumers and voters behaved in the exact same way. This "complaint iceberg," Heskett explained, "contained many clues to service improvements out of sight to management. . . . If the iceberg exists for complaints, it is even more pronounced for compliments and constructive suggestions, for which consumers often have less incentive to communicate." Think of how much useful information you could obtain by increasing feedback by even a few more percent!

When starting up PlanetFeedback several years later, I conducted research that found that only one in twenty-five consumers are inclined to give feedback. I also found that, much as for the voters I had observed in California, the reasons most consumers don't give feedback are lack of time, inconvenience, difficulty making contact, cynicism, and distrust of the fleeting "feedback moment." In my mind, these reasons were like a corroded pipe that just needed a good unclogging.

The Web and the Watercooler

PlanetFeedback was all about breaking down barriers to feedback. Luckily for me, the Web was quickly becoming a better low-barrier-to-entry feedback platform than I could ever have dreamed. With e-mail response forms, two-way message boards, and online communities, blogs, podcasts, social networks, and video sharing, feedback was soon flowing through the pipes with a force of a tsunami.

But the catch is that most feedback isn't going directly to the companies. With the vast peer-to-peer networks proliferating on the Web, most conversations occur outside the company's purview. Even on PlanetFeedback, a site explicitly created to send feedback to companies, I quickly learned that the biggest motivation for sharing feedback was to be "heard" by other consumers, not to get a company response. In fact, most consumers cynically assumed that companies simply didn't care and wouldn't respond anyway. But they used our site because they found emotional gratification in sharing their experiences with others. They found that posting a letter would generate dozens of responses from other consumers, and this was much more immediate and satisfying than waiting for the company to reply. Consumers who had problems with a wireless provider's customer service, for example, would quickly find common ground with other aggrieved users of that service. The ensuing conversation would amount to a form of emotional catharsis—a chorus of comments like "You too?" or "Oh, I've been there" or "Man, if only I could have warned you ahead of time!"

Such emotional connections lie at the heart of consumer-generated media. All those connected consumers out there aren't just interested in talking to you; they are far more interested in talking to one another. So what can you do to make sure your company doesn't miss out on what they are saying?

The first step is to learn what consumer-generated media looks like, who is creating it, and where to find it. The rest of this chapter will teach you how to do just that.

The Birth of CGM

Companies have long relied on traditional qualitative research in the form of focus groups, surveys, and polls to find out what consumers think. Sample groups of prescreened, prequalified consumers, typically representative subgroups of the relevant target market, work fine for providing basic insights and clues, but they have shortcomings. When guided, prompted, and asked overt questions, people may involuntarily conform to others' answers or respond according to what they think the moderator wants to hear rather than what they truly feel. More important, most qualitative survey methods involve multiple-choice methods, such as checking boxes, not open-ended discussion about real-life experiences.

But today, the Web allows forms of feedback that are unscripted and conversational, and thus a more accurate and candid look at consumers' attitudes and opinions. And what's more, it gives average people and consumers the tools and resources to enter the marketplace of ideas and commerce in ways never before imagined.

Even in the very early days of the Web, there were online communities called newsgroups, which allowed consumers to interact and communicate with one another on a wide range of topics. As technology improved, and more and more Americans gained home connections to the Internet, hundreds of thousands of other Internet forums, message boards, and communities proliferated, including countless industry-focused or interest-focused sites. Now, consumers can log on and see what millions of others are saying about the new Ford Taurus or the best brand of baby food.

With the advent of Really Simple Syndication (RSS), a method of Web publishing that allows any user to easily import information from one Web site to another, the number and breadth of online forums only grew. Soon came blogs, which use RSS technology to drive back-and-forth communication among multiple users. Because of their user-friendly format, unlimited linking capacity, and high search engine rankings, blogs soon became the most potent and popular vehicles for CGM.

BEYOND BLOGS

In recent years, the world of CGM has undergone a revolutionary shift from text to multimedia. The next generation of consumer-generated media is rapidly taking shape. Adopting the same rich-media formats we see in online advertising, CGM forums include photo-sharing and tagging sites such as Flickr, video-sharing sites such as Bebo and YouTube, multimedia social networks such as Facebook and MySpace, audio-streaming sites and podcasts, and moblogs, or mobile-enabled blogs, which let users post photos using their mobile phone cameras.

As we saw with the story of Vincent Ferrari and AOL in the introduction, podcasts, or audio media files that are distributed over the Web and can be played back on personal computers or on mobile devices such as iPods, allow consumers to record their negative experiences with customer service reps or tech support operators and post the recordings on their blogs or social networking pages for millions to hear.

The explosion in digital photography, too, has added a powerful form of expression to consumer testimonials. A hostile review of a General Motors car accompanied by a photo of an engine bursting into flames, for example, will obviously have more impact on consumers than a written commentary.

And then there's *video*. YouTube and the other video-sharing sites it has inspired have proven to be the ultimate platforms for the most sticky, viral, and incriminating CGM imaginable. For example, in June 2006, Comcast found itself in the middle of a viral firestorm when a guy named Brian Finkelstein came home to find a Comcast technician asleep on his couch. Making matters worse, the technician had fallen asleep waiting for Comcast's own customer support line to answer the phone. Finkelstein quickly took a video of the sleeping repairman and posted it to YouTube, where it was viewed by over 500,000 people within hours. The story was, of course, then picked up by bloggers, MSNBC, and several national newspapers; it continues to punish Comcast by showing up in search results.

Even as early as 2005, in the prehistoric era of CGM, two

popular videos proved credibility nightmares for the lock companies Kryptonite and Kensington when they were unleashed on the Web. One, originally posted on Engadget.com, showed how easy it is to pick a Kryptonite bike lock with an assortment of household objects, including a Bic pen. The other demonstrated how to break the Kensington lock on a laptop using a toilet paper roll, a ballpoint pen, and duct tape. Because of their novelty at the time, these videos proved particularly viral, prompting a firestorm among bloggers and a surge of negative publicity for both companies.

The point is, today, the cameras and microphones are always on and rolling. And companies are getting their close-ups.

FROM INTIMATE CONNECTIONS TO "SOCIAL NETWORKS"

Consumer-to-consumer communication has reached ever more viral levels through social networks. Sites such as MySpace, Six Degrees, Facebook, LinkedIn, and LiveJournal, where users create communities and can invite their friends, cohorts, colleagues, acquaintances, and sometimes even total strangers to join, can spread information faster than a kindergartener spreads chicken pox thanks to their limitless capacity for connections. For example, I'm a member of the LinkedIn professional network. I have about 300 primary contacts but thousands in my extended network. So if I post a comment about an experience with T-Mobile's customer service, for example, it can be viewed not only by the thousands in my extended network but by the thousands in each of those people's extended networks, and so on. This is why social networks have such huge implications—both positive and negative—for companies. If an entire extended social network of ten thousand sees a post that the new L'Oréal hair product is the best on the market, it will certainly mean more sales. On the other hand, someone posting a photo of himself vomiting after eating at a fast-food chain can only hurt the chain's business. And this gets at the very heart of why credibility is so important—credible companies get rewarded by CGM, while companies that are not credible get skewered by it.

Consumers with Megaphones: Who Are They?

There is no single author of this new media—we're all writing the story together. And while, as we have seen, every consumer has the power to make himself or herself heard, certain groups of people do wield more CGM influence than others. These highly engaged consumers have a number of amazingly simple yet powerful ways of creating a cacophony via their blogs, Web sites, social networking pages, and more. Unlike the average consumer, who might be content sharing an opinion about a company or product with a handful of friends, these CGM influencers won't stop until they have conveyed their opinions to an electronic audience of thousands, who in turn cross-pollinate this information like bees. However the exchange may flower, it has a profound impact on a company's credibility.

As we saw in the cases of Vincent Ferrari and AOL, and San

Diego Johnny and Wal-Mart, single unknown bloggers now wield the power to galvanize public outrage and undermine multibillion-dollar corporations. But high-profile bloggers are even more powerful. Bloggers such as Steve Rubel (www .micropersuasion.com), Arianna Huffington (www.huffington post.com), and Robert Scoble (scobleizer.com) are credible and influential even before opening their mouths, both by dint of their background, credentials, and expertise, and by virtue of their having built up a critical mass of recognition and acceptance in the blogosphere. Their influence is amplified by how extensively networked they are; these mega-bloggers have hundreds of other blogs linked to their sites.

Companies need to monitor these influencers vigilantly because, as I learned in my experience in the California Senate, they often reflect the views and opinions of countless others, whose voices are not always heard. Companies should recognize that, for every Arianna Huffington, there are millions of Random Joes lurking in every corner of the world who share their views.

Companies need to pay even more attention to these influencers now that the mainstream media is increasingly focusing its lens on the blogging world. Remember Vincent Ferrari and his call with AOL? What about Bob Garfield and his crusade against Comcast? True, all these stories initially proliferated via the Web, but it wasn't until they were picked up by the national mainstream media that they reached their full impact. Now that television, newspapers, and magazines are extending the reach of CGM beyond the world of the

Web, it's even more essential that companies tap into these online conversations—before they hit prime time.

Here are profiles of four of the most active and influential types of CGM creators and where to find them.

TECHNO TEEN

Several years ago, I conducted a "Consumer-Generated Media Engagement Monitor" study, which yielded some useful information about which consumers are creating and using these new forms of media to spread their ideas, opinions, and influence. The study found, not surprisingly, that consumers who create Web content are also active users of other technologies, from digital cameras and BlackBerries to the latest computer software. It found that consumers who use iPods and MP3 players, download music and multimedia files, and shop online are more likely than others to author a blog, participate in online discussions, and have large and active online social networks.

So it's no surprise that today's teens, computer-literate since preschool, lead all other groups in overall CGM creation. Nearly 50 percent of teens send photos via their cell phones; 45 percent have experimented with or created a blog, and over 10 percent have subscribed to an RSS feed. Teens are twice as likely to have posted content on their own Web sites and 37 percent more likely to post original comments on other Web sites than all other age segments.

Meanwhile, well over 100 million people now have My-Space pages, and most of them are teens. As Janet Kornblum put it in a recent *USA Today* article, "Forget the mall. Forget the movies. Forget school. Forget even AOL. If you're a teen in America today, the place to be is the social networking site MySpace." And more recently, Facebook has been all the rage, with over 2 million new users signing up each week (as of late 2007), no small percentage of which are teens.

It's obvious that CGM creation and consumption is becoming part of everyday life for today's teens. As new digital devices seem to be hitting the market virtually every day (as in the case of the iPhone), tech-savvy consumers can create, share, and distribute their own content with ever-increasing ease. And these new technologies—mobile phones, personal assistants, digital music players—heavily embraced by teens are serving as important proxies for broader CGM behavior. So if you want to find out what is being said about your company or brand online, listening to teens is a good place to start.

The type of teen I call the Techno Teen, in particular, is a voracious information gatherer, opinion disseminator, and social networker. Techno Teens are wired to multiple platforms. They can name a dozen or so "must read" blogs, many on the cutting edge of current trends. Their communication style is short and sweet—filled with initialisms such as "IMHO" (in my humble opinion), which are nearly impossible for anyone born before the Reagan administration to decipher. They have hundreds of friends on MySpace or Facebook, and their pages are filled with content galore: photos, bookmarks, videos, overflowing message boxes. What's more, their favorite products—CDs, movies, electronics—are bookmarked on their social media sites. At the same time, they aren't shy about saying which products they think stink. When the newest cell phone, or digital camera, or MP3 player comes out, Techno Teens are the first to use it, and the first to rant or rave about it on MySpace or their favorite blogs. "This notion of teens being in touch all the time, anytime, is striking," says Lee Rainie, founding director of the Pew Internet & American Life Project. "Their conversations never end and anytime a sort of new input enters their lives—gossip or real news—they have the capacity to broadcast it to a wider group."

In May 2007, for example, the Techno Teen Bryan Martorana organized a daylong gas boycott by asking all his Facebook friends to visit the "Don't Pump Gas" Web page he had created. Facebook took the campaign viral, and by the day before the boycott, more than ten thousand people had visited the site. Martorana's boycott didn't achieve quite the effect he'd hoped (one day away from the pumps doesn't really conserve much gas), but the widespread media pickup— from the *New York Post* to the Waterloo–Cedar Falls, Iowa, *Courier* and KVOA-TV News in Tucson—showed that a teen with a Facebook account and a cause can create a real stir if he or she has a mind to.

But teens aren't the only ones churning out CGM by the truckload. Three other consumer types are major players in the CGM world. They are the Power Mom, the Gadget Guy, and the Radical Flamethrower. Here is a closer look.

POWER MOM (OR DAD)

The Power Mom (or Dad) may not be as tech-savvy as her (or his) teenage offspring, but when it comes to CGM, she is just as influential. Power Moms, who often balance their careers with parenting, have little free time and therefore have no choice but to connect and communicate in the most efficient way possible. Bound by a sense of community and responsibility, Power Moms will go out of their way to tell fellow parents and other consumers about their opinions on or experiences with products or companies—particularly those, like cold medicines or diapers or minivans, that have to do with the health and safety of their families. They are likely to blog, chat online, share digital pictures, and even publish or be quoted in an online newsletter or on someone's Web site about a product. They actively conduct Internet research before they buy, and they are significantly more likely than average consumers not only to buy online but then to post detailed comments about their purchases and purchasing experiences.

Beth Theve is a mother of three in Ohio and a classic Power Mom. The leader of her daughter's Girl Scout troop, she balances a busy household with part-time community relations work. As an early member of MySpace as well as the fast-growing 10-million-member LiveJournal social network, Beth is intimately tied to a vast and vocal community of online consumers, especially moms. On these networks, she frequently contributes opinions and commentary on everything from her McDonald's boycott and the latest DVDs to the quality of service at local restaurants. Power Moms like Beth are well connected and outspoken, and their opinions are everywhere. If you run a company, sell a product, or offer a service, you want to stay in their good graces.

GADGET GUY

The Gadget Guy was the first one on the block with a broadband Internet connection, and he leaves a digital trail everywhere. If some cool new digital toy or technological breakthrough comes out, he's either the first to buy it or the first to know how to use it. If he happened to live in New York City in June 2007, he probably stood outside the Apple store for hours waiting for the release of the new iPhone. His daily reading material consists of dozens of Web sites, online forums, and blogs that help him stay ahead of the key trends, and he is usually the first one to post a review about new software or a new gizmo. He is proud, detailed, and extremely devoted to exposing "the truth" about a company or product. The Gadget Guy is fully versed in the power and influence of online video, and he is quick to capture a bad consumer experience on film and immediately post it on YouTube. He knows how to exploit his savvy to make a point.

The Gadget Guy is also a search engine animal. He'll search, research, and analyze every topic, from health and medical issues to electronics, entertainment, video games, pet products, computers, telecommunications, and more. And because he's so tech savvy, he knows how to track down most any information available, then add his own input.

Gadget Guys are increasingly being courted by advertisers and marketers who appreciate their depth of influence in the marketplace. But this courting is a double-edged sword, because the Gadget Guy's loyalty can be won only if your product actually works and measures up to expectations. Indeed, alienate the Gadget Guy at your peril.

Ted McConnell is a typical Gadget Guy. He knows what's hot, what's not, and what's coming right around the corner. As a director of innovation at Procter & Gamble, he's either tested most products himself or read dozens of reviews of them. When McConnell posts online about products he likes or dislikes, his comments are focused, detailed, and steeped in authority. Indeed, much of Ted's social currency among his personal network is tied to his authoritative knowledge about technology and gadgets.

RADICAL FLAMETHROWER

Then there's the Radical Flamethrower. Perhaps the most vocal of all the CGM influencers, this highly engaged consumer doesn't necessarily have the tech savvy of Gadget Guy, but he (or she) does understand better than anyone else how technology can be exploited to spread information and make himself (or herself) heard.

The Radical Flamethrower understands that aggregating like-minded consumer voices on a common topic can amplify a message to dramatically increase the odds of being noticed. For example, the Radical Flamethrower might take a video clip from a CEO's speech on protecting the environment and mix it up with less flattering footage of environmental abuse perpetrated by the company, then put it on YouTube. Or the Radical Flamethrower might record a horribly managed call-center transaction, edit it a bit for entertainment value, and put it up on the Web to shame and embarrass the company.

Vincent Ferrari, the guy who recorded his infuriating conversation with the AOL customer service representative, then spread it wide on the Web, is a classic example of a Radical Flamethrower. So is Ben Popken, editor of Consumerist.com, a Gawker media blog. Unabashedly pro-consumer (its tagline is "Shoppers bite back"), the site posts letters, complaints, photos, and videos that take companies to task for a host of wrongdoings. And thanks to Popken's (and others') take-no-prisoners reporting and commentary, this blog has not only a huge online audience but also an incredible spillover into mainstream media; it gets tens of thousands of hits a day, and reporters from all over the country routinely consult it to supplement or research their own stories.

Radical flamethrowers like Popken know how to create sticky, viral messages that resonate—and they know how to take full advantage of the Internet megaphone. All in all, they are pretty dangerous to ignore.

Consumers and the Purchase Cycle

Creators of CGM wield influence in different ways, depending on whether they are in a pre-shopping, shopping, or post-shopping mode. Before a purchase, consumers may have a long list of general questions to ask other consumers about a product, but because they haven't yet purchased the product, they rarely bring a deep level of expertise to their online messages. Consumers who have actually purchased and used products obviously bring more relevant experience and authority to the CGM table. When evaluating CGM, you need to understand what stage in the purchase cycle the consumer is coming from. The following six consumer types—pre-shoppers, brand ambassadors, brand detractors, gatherers, loiterers and freeloaders, and impostors and megaphonies—represent the stages in the cycle.

Pre-shoppers are still in "consideration" mode, and they make use of search engines and CGM venues to find out about products before they buy them. Online product reviews—whether in the form of written comments, photos, or video testimonials—exert a big influence on pre-shoppers.

Brand ambassadors are satisfied consumers who share their passion and authority about a product or company with other consumers through CGM. They tend to post comments on product blogs and write reviews on sites like Amazon. They can have a meaningful impact on the purchase behavior of other consumers. Apple users, for example, tend to be brand ambassadors. They use and absolutely love Apple products, and this comes across loud and clear in their CGM. And their brand loyalty typically gets taken into account by pre-shoppers.

Brand detractors also have relevant experience with a company or brand, but they are dissatisfied to the point where they feel the urge, sometimes the ethical duty, to warn other consumers. Brand detractors tend to be highly vocal, and their influence is increasing as better communication tools emerge. As we have seen, brand detractors' comments can incalculably hurt a business or damage a brand. Dissatisfied employees or former employees also fall into this category, and their comments are even more harmful because consumers tend to trust what employees say about companies they worked for.

Gatherers may or may not have relevant experience with products, but they play an increasingly important role in the marketplace, especially with the explosion of blogs. By aggregating a number of blogs on gaming into a single blog, for example, the gatherer's site may become a de facto destination for pre-shoppers of video games. Therefore, the gatherers' power lies in the CGM they choose to aggregate. In this example, if a gatherer chooses not to include any positive customer reviews of Grand Theft Auto IV, pre-shoppers who visit the site may assume that only bad reviews exist and be deterred from buying it.

Loiterers and freeloaders have no intention of buying products, but they still like to talk about them. Their commentary may have some impact on others' purchasing behavior, but it's far less influential than comments from people who have firsthand experience with a company or product. A lot of consumers use comparison shopping sites such as Shopzilla, PriceGrabber, and FatWallet to browse prices and offerings. They may do so to educate themselves for future purchases or to satisfy an urge to "window-shop."

Like consumers who spend the whole day at the mall but don't buy a thing, loiterers look, but they often don't buy. No matter what the driving force, a site full of loiterers is not the best place to advertise a brand message.

Impostors and megaphonies are essentially shills that companies or marketers pay to seed commentary about a particular brand. Impostors sometimes succeed in shaping consumer opinion or building buzz around a new company or product. But this practice can backfire. If it's discovered that a consumer is a paid agent of a company, trust and credibility plummets, for both the impostor and the company.

It's worth taking a moment to offer a few examples of impostors to underscore their real threat to a company's credibility. A few years ago one of Sony's interactive agencies, Zipatoni, set up a blog supposedly by a kid named Charlie who was trying to convince his friend Jeremy's parents to buy Jeremy a Portable Sony Playstation for Christmas. But when curious consumers discovered that the blog's domain owner was a marketing company employed by Sony, Sony was forced to take the blog down amid a hailstorm of bad publicity. Although sales of the PSP didn't suffer significantly, the incident raised plenty of questions about Sony's credibility. The incident also raised important questions about the damage ad agencies can inflict—often unwittingly—on a company's credibility.

McDonald's toed the line between a clever PR stunt and deceptive marketing in 2005, when Super Bowl viewers were treated to ads that featured a French fry with a purported likeness of Abraham Lincoln. McDonald's then set up a Web site that featured a blog by the person who had supposedly found the Lincolnesque French fry. All aboveboard, except for the fact that the person wasn't real—he was invented by marketers in an attempt to drive traffic to the promotional Web site. One could argue that if a commercial about a "Lincoln fry" directs you to a Web site, you don't have much of a hold on reality anyway, but still, McDonald's went so far as to fabricate a story, create a false persona, and post fake comments on a fake blog. And many consumers were duly outraged. Imagine "Honest" Abe promoting such trickery!

The power shift from companies to consumers has been driven largely by how intensively consumers are now researching brands. Today, the term *market research* has been turned on its head; consumers research marketers and companies, not just the other way around. Consumers scrutinize every message, angle, or positioning spin. Indeed, as Procter & Gamble's A. G. Lafley is known to say, "The consumer is boss."

You now know how to identify the key types of CGM influencers. But you can't assess the impact of CGM on your company if you don't know how to read and measure it. You have to figure out not only who's talking but what they're saying, and why. If you want to have credibility, you need a system for gathering, measuring, and responding to CGM on every front. In the next chapter, I'll tell you how you can accomplish exactly that.

Chapter 3

Measuring CGM

Before the Internet, word of mouth was invariably localized, incidental, and fleeting. A dissatisfied consumer could perhaps convince the members of his or her immediate circle to stop shopping at Wal-Mart, or to buy hybrid vehicles, but any given opinion, rumor, or experience would generally dissipate with the wind. Online word of mouth, by contrast, is far more tenacious. Thanks to the archived nature of the Internet, consumer-generated media leaves a lasting digital trail that provides unobstructed entry into the minds of millions of consumers having conversations in real time.

The good news is that these conversations can be monitored, tracked, traced, and measured in ways that allow companies to tune in, join in, and learn what consumers really think—before it's too late. This chapter will show you how.

Tools for Measuring CGM

Whether you hire a major firm like Nielsen Online, Cymfony/TNS, Umbria, or BuzzLogic, or use any of the various free tools available online, you should be religiously mining the Web to understand what CGM is saying about your brand. Without proper measuring models in place, business owners, executives, managers, or anyone with a stake in a company and its products is functioning in an information vacuum. Fortunately, the blogosphere's organization allows companies to decode the content fairly easily. Link structure, blog citations, and trackbacks (bloggers are notified when anyone links to their posts) paint a clear picture. Even the free video sites offer a host of excellent free metrics. CGM is so easily traceable, there's no excuse for not knowing what your customers are saying about your company.

So, how exactly can you quantify and measure CGM? One way companies can collect CGM is by using content-mining tools to sweep the Internet and drill deep for themes, contexts, complaints, actions and reactions related to a given company or brand. Like search engines, content-mining engines crawl the ever-growing online content, index and categorize that content, and neatly rank, organize, and present the results. In addition to measuring the sheer volume of buzz, content-mining tools can identify key phrases, words, and concepts; analyze links; detect the nature and strength of sentiment in text; and identify and analyze relevant messages from a variety of online sources.

Of course, not all businesses can afford full-service analytic tools like those we use at Nielsen Online. Luckily, a number of excellent free tools are available to help companies track and measure consumer conversations about virtually anything—specific marketing and ad campaigns, product launches, news events, and industry fluctuations. These tools and services are getting better and better at aggregating multimedia sources and providing a more complete and nuanced picture of the consumer conversation. And as we've seen, listening and responding to consumer conversations is what credibility is all about.

GETTING STARTED

I always encourage clients to start a blog as a way to learn how to track readership, feed subscriptions, map trackbacks, index blog search engines, and more. To set up a personal blog, I suggest starting with a very basic and user-friendly blog publishing tool, such as TypePad, WordPress, or Blogger. Most of these are free or cost very little. My TypePad account provides all the functions and capability I need for as many blogs as I want to write for about fifteen dollars a month.

I also encourage newbies to establish a simple blog "reader" through Google or Yahoo! or subscribe to one of the more sophisticated "blog feed" services, like Bloglines. These services automatically deliver the most updated content (feeds) from all the blogs you subscribe to into your blog mailbox like e-mail. Blog feeds make it easier to sift through a ton of relevant content while supplying excellent fodder for writing your own blog.

You can also use your own blog to practice indexed searching, which means searching basic word matches. Entering "McDonald's" or "McDonald's and transfat," for example, would return all relevant blog comments using those terms. This is a very accessible, straightforward way of getting a quick read on an issue related to your company or brand.

Here are eight free tools for performing an indexed search, and how to use them.

Technorati Blog Search: Technorati is a free search engine for searching blog content. On Technorati.com, if you type your company's name in the search box, it will deliver up-to-the-minute commentary about your company from over 80 million blogs. Technorati allows you to set up alerts when something is written about your company, review "most popular" lists in a variety of categories, and quickly glean most popular searches across the blogosphere. This information is invaluable, as the top search queries convey what is uppermost in consumers' minds. If a big story is breaking about an issue relevant to your company or industry, the number of search queries related to that story reflect how much interest consumers have in the topic.

Technorati also organizes the blogosphere by tags, key words or phrases that catalog a blog's content. Tags work kind of like entries in a book index, helping a reader pinpoint exactly where to look for specific information, but they are interactive. Tags also function as links to other Web sites with the same tags—like a cross-reference feature. By efficiently cataloging a blog's content, tags make it easier for other consumers to find that content. The blogger determines the tags, but many blog search engines have lists of preexisting tags that bloggers can put to work. For my personal blog, Dosbebes, for example, I can tag my content with "parenting" or "twins" or "awake at 4:00 A.M."

On Technorati, you can also request automatic e-mails that link you to blog entries containing certain key words. You can use alerts to track references to yourself, your company, or your competitors. One caveat: If you set too many alerts, you'll soon find yourself overwhelmed. Most companies, for example, receive hundreds of blog references daily, the majority of which they don't have time to read. An advantage of paid Web-monitoring services is that they send alerts only when the volume of buzz hits significant levels. That way you don't have to read every post, but if buzz volume suddenly spikes, you will know immediately.

Nielsen BlogPulse: Nielsen also offers a free blog analytic and search tool known as BlogPulse. BlogPulse conducts quick and easy searches across more than 75 million blogs. With its Trend Charts feature, users can create their own graphs that plot buzz about specific search terms (issues, people, companies, brands, sports, et cetera) for up to three time parameters—one month, two months, or six months. These charts provide managers with a quick read on the direction the buzz seems to be going and can help them spot spikes in buzz activity on any number of topics—a new commercial, a product launch, an announcement, an event, or (hopefully not) bad news, like a corporate scandal or product recall.

Google Blog Search: Google Blog Search doesn't include as many fancy features as sites like Technorati, but it gets the job done. It searches every blog going back to June 2005 that publishes a site feed (either RSS or Atom). Google allows you to search easily by topic, date range, and more. It also allows you to set alerts against just about any topic or theme that might show up in the blogosphere. If your company name appears on several blogs in a given day, Google will aggregate all the relevant posts and send them to you in a single e-mail.

IceRocket: IceRocket searches across not only blogs but also MySpace pages, news sources, images, and more recently, video. Like BlogPulse, IceRocket offers trend charts that allow users to plot two variables along a common buzz curve. If you type in "Pepsi" and "Coke," for example, you'll see a chart showing the total number of times those brands were mentioned over a given period. IceRocket also ranks "most popular" blog entries and topics.

YouTube and Google Video Search: With the growing popularity of online video, monitoring the video space is increasingly important. Sites like Google Video and YouTube allow you to search their vast databases of content for mention of your company or product. For example, if you type "Burger King" into YouTube, you'll get over 4,600 results. The first video that appeared last time I checked was "Burger

King Outsources," showing how the fast-food chain outsources order taking to remote call centers. On YouTube, once you find the relevant videos, you can see the number of views and read the comments, video responses, and various ratings related to the video. Users can sort the videos by "relevance," "view count," or "date added."

Flickr and Photo Search: Similarly, you can obtain invaluable information by searching across the millions of photos posted on major photo-sharing sites like Flickr. These services allow users to tag photos, which aids the search and discovery process. For example, in a presentation to the Cincinnati Chamber of Commerce, I demonstrated how, by simply typing in "Cincinnati" and "landmarks," the chamber could get a pretty good idea of what spots in the city are most photographed—and hence probably most visited—by tourists.

Ratings and Review Search: Well before the explosion of blogs, online videos, and MySpace, ratings and review sites had an impact on consumer purchase behavior—and they still do. You can easily search major review sites, like Epinions .com or CNET, to read reviews of your company, product, or brand. These reviews offer very credible feedback, because they are written by consumers who have actually used the product.

That said, like anything on the Internet, user reviews must be taken with a grain of salt. Some people do have agendas, and the Internet has given people a much bigger—and often anonymous—soapbox to stand on. If one person writes that Verizon Wireless service drops too many calls, it should be duly noted. If fifty people say so, it should set off warning bells and alarms for Verizon.

Community-Based News Sites: Community-based news Web sites like Digg or Reddit, Fark, and del.icio.us allow users to select, share, bookmark, and discuss whatever news, videos, and podcasts are relevant to them. These sites serve as an excellent form of CGM analytics because they provide a window into which issues are popular, and which have the most traction. Since these sites rely on the aggregate preferences of users or the "wisdom of the crowds," they have huge implications for companies. Brand-related topics that rise fast on Digg typically spell either great news or ugly trouble. A smart tactic for managers and business owners looking to stay on top of issues is to periodically review their standing on these sites.

WHAT SPECIFICALLY CAN YOU MEASURE?

The amount of measurable information on the Web is nearly unlimited, but not everything that is measurable is meaningful. Companies need to focus on the CGM that answers the most relevant questions and informs the best decision making across all arms of the organization. The following is a list of key CGM metrics, some available via the free tools, and most if not all available through the premium monitoring services—and what they can tell you:

KEY METRIC	WHAT IT TELLS YOU
Volume	How many comments are there about your company?
Reach	What is the depth of exposure? How widely are the comments viewed by others?
Issue	What specific issues are being discussed?
Sentiment	To what extent are messages favorable or unfavorable?
Emotion	How do consumers feel about your company?
Dispersion	How viral is the issue or conversation?
Source	Where is conversation occurring?
Author	Who is the source? Are his or her comments credible?

One other note about the free services, and this extends to Google. All of them are getting far better at aggregating multimedia sources. Technorati and Google, for example, do a nice job bringing together all the relevant content related to this author, Pete Blackshaw. If you punch in my name, you'll see my blog posts, my "authority" level, my videos, my photos, and more. Some would argue this is "too much information," but such is the world we live in.

1. Volume and Reach: How Much Brand Buzz Is Out There?

To determine the net *volume* of conversation taking place about a brand, you can use the trend chart features on services like BlogPulse. These tools conduct a broad sweep across blogs for single or multiple search terms and create graphs that visually track the volume of buzz over time. Blog-Pulse can also be used to compare your buzz volume with that of your top competitors, as seen in the graph. Understanding total volume is a good way to start an analysis of CGM; managers, CMOs, and CEOs are usually amazed at the sheer number of comments that turn up about their brands.

Monitoring firms can sweep all CGM venues—blogs, message boards, ratings and review sites, video-sharing sites, and more—and measure the volume of buzz for key words or topics. These companies can also marry this data with other relevant data such as sales volume, media spending, or internal feedback, and even combine this data with hands-on experience with analysts or account representatives. In other words, these firms can combine CGM with other research to provide a more holistic picture of what is going on.

Let's say you work at McDonald's and you want to see whether or not the promotion of the new "food, nutrition, and fitness" program is working. You could search for conversations about McDonald's, then categorize the results into topics such as transfat, new menu options, free pedometers,

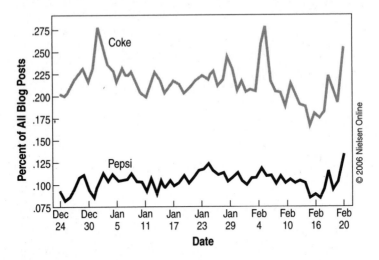

Here's a graph showing CGM as measured by total volume in the blogosphere. One-tenth of 1 percent of 40 million blogs contain references to Pepsi, compared with two-tenths of a percent for Coke. Is this a big deal? It may not seem like it at first, but if you do the math, you'll see that this extra tenth of a percent amounts to 40,000 more blog posts about Coke. In other words, even a fraction of a percent of buzz volume can have a huge impact.

et cetera. These counts can be refreshed daily, in some cases hourly, providing managers with a sense of how buzz is fluctuating. In theory, companies could do this on their own, but self-measurement requires expertise on analyzing trends and a grasp of Web code that a lot of folks don't have. In addition, these undertakings are very time and eyeball intensive, because they return a massive amount of information with no road map on how to interpret it. So unless your company is Web savvy enough to accurately and efficiently evaluate all the available information, and can afford all the necessary labor investment to view, filter, and interpret the results, you may want to hire a firm to handle the more complex levels of CGM analysis.

It's also possible to measure the degree to which volume is growing. Volume may grow as a result of a marketing initiative, a talk-worthy product hitting the market, or a nasty rumor enveloping your company. Take Apple, for example. Its buzz volume spiked tremendously when word spread that the company was launching the revolutionary iPhone. Same with Nintendo: Buzz volume increased during the first holiday season its new Wii was available.

Reach is as critical a measure of CGM as it is of traditional media. Quite simply, the further the reach, the greater the impact. Reach is harder to calculate than volume because you have to consider not only the number of eyeballs but the power and influence of those eyeballs. A blog, for example, may have low readership, but if its core readers are influential—say, reporters or politicians—that blog will have considerable reach.

The CGM influencers I discussed in Chapter 2, for example, are likely to have greater reach than your average Joe. But there are other factors. The reach of a CGM creator's influence can be measured through a number of variables, including

- Size of social network
- Number of consumers who consistently link to that consumer's content

- RSS feeds into that consumer
- Background, experience, and authority of that consumer
- Degree to which that consumer has access to the mainstream media and other sources
- Depth of engagement by other influencers, especially media writers, on that person's content
- Actual readership
- Citations by other media sources
- Timing: Consumers who are first to have a particular experience accrue situational influence.

Google News can help you figure out how much reach a blog post has because it can show you whether the post has spilled over into the major mainstream media. Even measuring spillover into television coverage is getting easier; a growing percentage of TV content, especially TV news coverage, is being reindexed on Google. If you type "Ben Popken" (of The Consumerist) into any major search engine, you'll see that he's frequently quoted or referenced in newspapers, TV coverage, online publications, and of course other blogs. That is spillover.

You can calculate the reach of the buzz about your company using another free BlogPulse tool called Conversation Tracker. This feature charts how far any conversation—searchable by blog posts, links/URLs, or search terms/key words—has traveled on the Web.

For many companies, reach needs to be constantly recalculated, whether through technology or simply by reexamining the ranking of key search results on Google. The "digital trail" of CGM is revealed in lockstep with search queries. The net reach over 2007's pet food recall, for example, continues to grow because when people search for articles or blog posts relating to the incident, all the sites containing negative comments and consumer concern over tainted pet food are reintroduced in the search results. In the past, even a huge recall would eventually disappear from the news cycle and people would forget about it. Now, with a few simple keystrokes, it can be revived and relived in all its glory, courtesy of Google and other major search engines.

2. ISSUE: WHAT ARE CONSUMERS TALKING ABOUT, AND WHY?

You can use the indexed search tool on Technorati, Google Blog Search, Blog Pulse, or any of the other free tools I've described to find out how much buzz there is about specific issues surrounding your company or product. You can also go to sites like Digg, del.icio.us, and The Humm to see exactly what kinds of conversations are surrounding the issues. This is particularly useful because pinpointing the issues consumers are talking about can provide enormous insight on which business processes you should be focusing on. If Toyota, for example, learned that 20 percent of commentary about its vehicles had to do with gas mileage, 10 percent had to do with style, and 5 percent was specifically centered on a recent Tundra advertising campaign, the company could infer that consumers care more about fuel efficiency than they do about product design or flashy new commercials. Or, as shown in the graph, if a theme park holding company finds that there is more buzz about crowds and attendance than there is about attractions, it can assume that visitors care more about having to stand in long lines than they do about checking out the newest roller coaster. This kind of information helps companies direct their resources toward the things consumers care about most.

Dissecting the data by issue can also help you diagnose problems, which informs decision making. If Sprint, for example, determines that 30 percent of blog posts about the company are complaints about billing practices, this is a clear indication that it should take a long, hard look at its billing system. Finding out about a billing problem is critical, because billing in general stirs high levels of consumer emotion and, hence, word of mouth; in fact, at PlanetFeedback we learned that billing was the most viral of all issues across the major cell phone carriers. When confronted with a billing error, consumers had a high propensity to post their letters online and copy others on their correspondence. So if a carrier knows that poor billing procedures are creating most of the company buzz *and* that billing buzz has a high propensity to spread, the company would do well to take extra measures to refine billing practices.

A company can also learn a lot from mapping words or

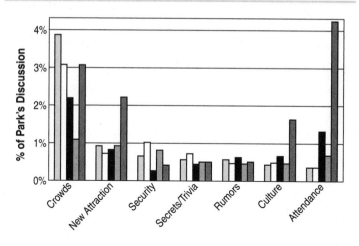

This graph shows how CGM breaks down by key issue against specific audience segments.

phrases commonly associated with its products or brands through advanced text and content mining. This process uses algorithms to identify key phrases and words, detect the nature and strength of sentiment in text, classify and categorize data, and extract specific facts from a variety of online sources. Some of this analysis can be done at a light level for free, but if you want a more detailed picture, you are probably best served by a more sophisticated filter. Most of the premium text-mining companies have invested a great deal into developing advanced algorithms to sort out certain types of content, reduce redundancy, or even, in some cases, filter out spam.

One fascinating brand-association map drawn from consumer-generated media on Nike looked like this.

In a brand-association map such as this one, the terms closest to the brand center are those mentioned most frequently and in closest proximity to the reference to the company. A company may also look at the proximity of its name to those of its competitors—if, for example, Adidas is more frequently mentioned alongside Nike than is Skechers, we can assume Adidas is a closer competitor. Another good measure of CGM is how frequently a company is associated with

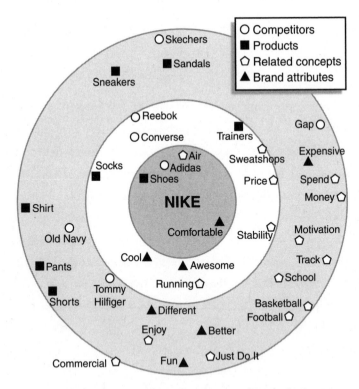

Nielsen Online brand-association map (BAM) of Nike

various product categories. In the case of Nike, this analysis produces a fascinating and subtle nuance: Why, for example, do consumers appear to talk more about Nike in the context of socks than of sneakers? Looking deeper into the story the CGM provides might offer new insights about the company's strategy.

Finding out which key words or phrases are most often associated with a company is also useful. Nike managers should be pleased that the adjectives *cool, comfortable, awesome,* and *different* are often attributed to their brand. But they may want to pay close attention to the fact that the word *better* is mentioned less frequently—this suggests they could be doing a better job of convincing consumers that their products are superior to the competition.

What keeps Nike's senior executives up at night is that the word *sweatshops* circulates close to the center. The fact that *sweatshops* consistently shows up in search results for Nike-related queries indicates that, despite the company's PR efforts, consumers continue to associate Nike with sweatshop labor. This may seem like a negative, but it may also reflect the company's attempt to fix the problem. Nike has recently pursued a more proactive strategy of publishing key data related to all its suppliers to address negative perceptions about its exploitation of cheap labor, so the presence of the association doesn't necessarily mean the brand is in trouble; it may mean that the brand is making progress in drawing consumers' attention to its PR efforts.

3. SENTIMENT: ARE THE COMMENTS ABOUT
MY COMPANY FAVORABLE?

Such ambiguities are one reason that companies' analysis of CGM should measure *sentiment*—whether consumers view the company, or the issues related to the company, positively or negatively. A strong brand association with environmental issues, or even the term *green*, for example, can cut both ways. For Toyota, *green* may very well reflect a positive validation of good practices and initiatives with hybrid vehicles. For Ford or GM, the same word may reflect intense and growing public frustration with the fact the automakers are not doing enough about the environment. Only by measuring the sentiment of the conversation can you tell whether certain associations are favorable or unfavorable toward your company.

Favorability is a critical part of the CGM monitoring mix because it helps you determine how well your brand is resonating with others. Customer service, for example, is a category that has high volume but is also often scarred by low sentiment or low favorability scores. By tracking favorability levels over long periods of time, companies can see the impact of certain advertising efforts or product improvements on consumer sentiment. Obviously, it's in the company's interest to have strong favorability scores.

Sentiment is far more difficult to measure with precision using the free tools, which is why larger marketers frequently opt for the paid monitor services. But all hope is not lost for the little guy. If you are just looking for a quick directional read on sentiment, you can glean it by looking at the tone of an initial thread or the favorability of the news story the blogger is citing. In the 2007 pet food and toy recall issues, for example, it wasn't difficult to determine the prevailing sentiment. Moreover, once you get used to using the free tools, you'll come to understand which bloggers are inherently positive and which are negative. Some bloggers, like Ben Popken of The Consumerist, are negative on almost every issue.

4. EMOTION: HOW DO CONSUMERS FEEL ABOUT YOU?

While *sentiment* refers to whether consumers feel positively or negatively about a company, *emotion* is tied to how strong these sentiments are, and what form they take. It's one thing to know that consumers feel generally unfavorable about your company's new pricing plan, for example, but it's even more useful to know whether they feel exploited and betrayed, or merely annoyed. Consumers' emotions have real financial implications. Most of the billions of archived consumer comments online stem from an emotional catalyst—positive or negative—which is all the more reason to measure emotion in CGM.

When I was at Procter & Gamble, emotion was everything. Our brand strategy for Bounty paper towels sought to identify Bounty as the "heroic household helper for moms." The core message was as emotional as it was rational—we wanted not only to convey the fact that Bounty was a superior product but also to foster an emotional association between Bounty and a loving mother's relationship with her kids. So we launched an ad campaign called "Little Kids, Big Spills" to reinforce the message that the Bounty brand was about maternal compassion and emotion. All the ads we produced had a similar formula: A very cute, innocent-looking kid unleashes a spill disaster; the mom initially freaks out but quickly smiles, knowing that Bounty, the "heroic household helper," is up to the task of saving the day. The Bounty campaign was pre-Internet, but it sparked a good deal of conversation among our target audience—moms—in focus groups and the like.

Emotion is central to word of mouth, and this is why companies need to understand and embrace consumers' emotional responses not only to their ad campaigns but also to their customer service, business practices, and products. Consumers reward not only brands that work and perform but companies that connect on an emotional level. In the age of CGM, credible companies are the ones that understand how emotions drive or kill business, and they have developed strategies to measure and manage consumers' emotional responses.

Measuring emotion across thousands, if not millions, of online conversations is one of the more complicated, yet exciting, endeavors in brand monitoring. The process is far from perfect, as emotion is laced with ambiguity, false positives, colloquial expressions, and more. At the very basic level, the most effective way to measure emotion is to scan raw text for statements or language that might indicate the author's opinion about a topic, brand, issue, or company. Easier said than done, of course, as it is often challenging to interpret how strong these positive or negative statements are. However, content-mining firms are developing increasingly reliable algorithms for determining strength of CGM emotion.

Beyond the basics of "positive or negative," it's possible to drill deeper. For example, advanced filters can be built to detect certain word associations and phrases, like the terms *outrage* or *betrayed,* which can be very telling. This is a very big deal because depth of emotion dictates depth of word of mouth. At PlanetFeedback, we found that consumers who felt betrayal or outrage over issues like "billing," for example, tended to have far higher word-of-mouth rates than consumers who felt mere annoyance.

5. Dispersion: How Viral Is What They're Saying?

Dispersion refers to the extent to which a comment, post, picture, or opinion spreads beyond its original source. Video has a particularly high dispersion factor, as consumers tend to share it with abandon. Bank of America learned this the hard way when an embarrassingly awful video song celebrating a recent merger was leaked from a meeting intended for employees and wound up on YouTube—announcing the merger to the country. In a matter of days, the video spread from YouTube to Stereogum to nearly every site across the Web. It was even picked up by VH1 and reported on in *The Wall Street Journal* and *The New York Times*. What started as something that seemed funny and cute turned into a real embarrassment—so much so that *Ad Age* magazine called it one of the worst gaffes of 2006.

In this age of instant dispersion, companies must be constantly on guard. In another "video seen round the world," a recent webcast on AT&T's Blue Room featured a Pearl Jam video in which, during a segue from "Daughter" to "Another Brick in the Wall," impromptu lyrics critical of George Bush were cut out. This created an instant freedom of speech maelstrom with AT&T squarely in the middle. Even though AT&T didn't directly do the censoring (a contract vendor in charge of making sure profanity didn't get aired was the culprit), AT&T has now become associated with censorship in the minds of countless subscribers.

When it comes to measuring dispersion—word of mouth might be a better term—all the free tools can provide a light level of analysis. Technorati, BlogPulse, and IceRocket allow you to follow the trail of links from one blog post to others, and BlogPulse's Conversation Tracker allows you to follow the trail of a blog post, a news article, a Web site link, or anything with a URL. For quick informal research, I use this tool to trace the dispersion of certain news articles. If you see lots of bloggers passing along a news article, or referencing the article in their posts, you can make a few assumptions about how viral the story has become. Any company trying to minimize bad publicity or quell a rumor obviously hopes for low-dispersion rates of CGM. But, for a brand launching a hot new product, the more dispersion, the better. The Internet has increased potential dispersion because, as we have seen, it can disseminate information faster and on a wider scale than traditional media.

6. SOURCE AND AUTHOR: WHO'S TALKING, WHERE, AND WHY?

It's critical to understand who is shaping the conversation about your brand, and whether the source and author beg more or less action from you. This is the one case where the credibility of the consumer matters. Do the people bad-mouthing your company have an ulterior motive? Could they be employed by a competitor? Are these complainers actually using your product, or are their comments secondhand? If complaints are coming from an untrustworthy source, it can often be better to ignore them than to dignify them with a response. If, however, they come from someone who has some real influence, you'll want to be quick to act. When it comes to decoding CGM, who is talking is often just as important as what they are saying.

To find out where—and by whom—a conversation about your company originated, you can use an advanced feature on blog feed services called trackbacking, which credits (tracks back) an idea to its original author/blogger. Analysis of CGM allows marketers and businesses to rank key bloggers or CGM creators by volume, category, or depth of influence. Tools like Nielsen Online's BlogPulse, IceRocket, Technorati, and Google Blog Search can measure a blogger's rank and number of weekly citations as well as the key words and phrases he or she most frequently uses. So if an influential blogger is talking about products or issues related to your company, you can determine how influential the commentary is, and what audiences it reaches.

Services like BlogPulse and Technorati also offer free profiles of bloggers that include posting behavior, linking activity, frequently blogged topics, ranking, range of influence, and any other information the bloggers provide. In some cases, you can even get information on an author's track record to better gauge his or her credibility. Technorati, for example, assigns an "authority" score, essentially the number of blogs linking to the particular blog for the last six months. And BlogPulse offers detailed looks at the "top 10,000" bloggers. So if you are losing sleep over a particular blogger, like Jeff Jarvis, you can type his blog address into the BlogPulse profile section and get a complete report on who typically reads or cites his blogs, or even the articles, bloggers, or periodicals he most frequently cites.

When analyzing CGM, it makes sense to pay attention to the comments from your company's core customer base. American Airlines, for example, listens to people who travel often for business. Whole Foods Market pays attention to the health-conscious. Pampers focuses on new parents. You get the point. An analysis is never complete until you get a handle on who is driving the conversation. In some cases, the analysis might merely confirm that the people who are talking are precisely the people you are hoping to reach and influence. In other instances, you might find that a whole new group of consumers is talking about your product or brand. A movie studio's marketing strategy might be aimed at teenage boys, for example, but if the online conversation suggests that women over thirty are actually excited about the movie, those women are an additional group the studio should target for similar movies or a sequel.

On the other hand, there is much to be learned from consumers who don't use your company's services or products. Wal-Mart, for instance, may want to look at CGM created by Target shoppers, or by women ages eighteen to twenty-four, or by Spanish speakers. Often, knowing what your company is doing to alienate certain groups can help you expand your customer base a lot better than listening to the positive things existing customers are saying. Either way, powerful and unique stories are sure to emerge.

A Little CGM Goes a Long Way

Like any traditional media, CGM influences the opinions, impressions, and most important, the purchasing behavior of other consumers. Measuring CGM, then, is just as important as scrutinizing ad copy, crafting a media pitch, or getting the packaging of a product just right—even more so, because of the viral nature of CGM and the speed at which it spreads. Consumer-generated media is not just a variation on media; in most cases it's *more* trusted, *more* credible, and even *more* permanent than traditional media.

Most companies know so little about what is being said about them online that even a little data can yield incredible rewards. And not just for marketers; every department in any company can benefit from tuning in to the consumer-generated discussion. So whether you are a manager, a call-center operator, a product researcher or designer, a sales rep, or a top executive, learning firsthand about consumers' real-time experiences provides invaluable insights into issues of the day or on the horizon. Free from the limitations imposed by the traditional focus group, CGM allows consumers to reveal their deepest emotions and most honest opinions, which carry the highest value for businesses striving to stay credible in a consumer-driven world.

Now that you know how to find, measure, and analyze all the online conversations about your company, you're ready to learn how to use this information to build credibility into everything your company does. In the remaining chapters, I'll show you how to put the six core credibility drivers to work throughout your organization.

The consumer is speaking . . . are you listening?

Chapter 4

Not All Marketers Are Liars: Marketing and Advertising with Credibility

T he days when marketers set the agenda are over. To-day's consumers don't want to be marketed to. But even though consumers increasingly control today's dialogue, marketers can still be part of the conversation. How? By making credibility a factor in all your marketing and advertising decisions. Ask yourself: What makes consumers feel valued and important? How can I reach consumers without interrupting or intruding on them? How can I put across my message in a way that conveys genuine respect? How can I invite meaningful participation and involvement? How can I create positive consumer-generated media on my company's behalf but not be perceived as inauthentic or overly manipulative? Here are some useful strategies.

Market with Transparency

Marketing *with* (not to) consumers works only in an atmosphere of complete honesty. Therefore, it's critical for companies to be completely transparent in their efforts to make CGM work for them. If companies are not up front with consumers, the consumers are likely to find out. This is the reality of today's online world. Bloggers, podcasters, social networkers, and the other CGM influencers I described in Chapter 2 will take companies to task if they are less than forthright in their claims.

In this era of accountability, stealth or undercover marketing will only bring grief and embarrassment to your company. Just ask Mazda. Several years ago, the carmaker's ad agency created a fictitious blog that purported to be by a Mazda customer. In addition to all the lavish praise for Mazda vehicles, the blog included three Mazda commercials claiming to be amateur, user-generated videos. Genuine bloggers smelled a rat a mile away and publicly pummeled Mazda all over the Web. To this day when you type "Mazda blog" in Google, it spits back the most vitriolic postings about the brand, from "Mazda blog comes unstuck" to "pretty lame," "stupid," and "a dumb-assed mistake."

Here's another example of why shill marketing never pays.

In late 2006 and early 2007, Wal-Mart's communications firm, Edelman PR, created a fake blog (or flog), to promote a program called "Wal-Marting Across America." Ostensibly, the blog was written by bona fide Wal-Mart fans, but in fact the authors were paid staffers of the PR company.

Bad idea. Faking anything is a recipe for a credibility disaster, and the venom poured across the blogosphere about Wal-Mart and Edelman once the deception was uncovered is proof positive of that. The disaster was especially grievous considering that CEO Richard Edelman and his firm helped, as *BusinessWeek* put it, "write the rulebook for companies trying to tap into the blogosphere." Not only had the Wal-Mart promotion gone amuck but Edelman's own credibility was under attack as well. Interestingly, rather than sit on the sidelines, Edelman PR proactively conceded error in the program and Richard Edelman himself actually contributed comments on a host of blogs. In particular, Edelman noted that social media "is a long-term education process for our people. Mistakes have been made but we are going to get up and ski the hill again and again until we get it right." In addition, Edelman and his firm proactively reasserted their commitment to the ethical guidelines developed by Word of Mouth Marketing Association (WOMMA), which put a high premium on transparency in identity in marketing communication.

But there is more to transparency than simply avoiding outright deception. Begin your company's transparency makeover by going down this checklist:

1. Do a DNA check.

How do consumers talk about your company? What is the tenor and tone of the commentary? Try to ensure that your communication with consumers is consistent with the focus of the external conversation. Often, a company's message is out of sync with the issues consumers are talking about on-line. For example, a consumer may pose a question on a blog that the company simply does not address in its ads, on its packaging, or on its Web site. This is a missed opportunity. Being transparent means being relevant. In order to market *with* consumers, companies need to constantly keep up with the questions consumers are asking and try to answer them openly and honestly.

2. DON'T BURY IT IN THE FINE PRINT.

Too many brands *claim* transparency but are actually hiding certain things by burying them in the fine print. Take the Internet phone company Vonage. While Vonage advertises a host of benefits, it hides many critical details about its service and fees in tiny type in hard-to-find reaches of its Web site. As a result, many consumers are unpleasantly surprised when they learn that the advertised benefits, such as advantageous pricing, caller ID, voice mail, call forwarding, and call wait-ing, are for new customers only, or that there are hidden fees added on to the base product. Consumers punished such lapses in credibility by leaving a digital trail of wrath and fury toward Vonage across the web.

Privacy policies and terms of service agreements on major Web portals are examples of information that often hides in fine print; consumers frequently forfeit such information be-cause these notices are long and difficult to read. The reality is that consumers simply don't have the patience to read the full text, and companies often bank on this and bury information there. One way to be more transparent is to communicate your "fine-print" message through a far more open medium, perhaps a video of the CEO explaining a company policy or a podcast of a customer describing an experience. Even if the information is not 100 percent flattering or positive, it's still better to be open and up front.

A great example is Progressive Insurance. Progressive lists competitors' insurance rates on its own Web site so that potential customers can compare quotes on the spot. This gutsy strategy may cost Progressive some business in the short term, but in the long run it lends the company massive credibility.

3. FACILITATE THE SEARCH.

Be sure the search engines on your Web site cover all the bases, and do so in a way that gets the most relevant information to the top of the search results. For example, if you type "social responsibility" on most corporate Web sites, either you don't get any hits or you get an irrelevant mess of random ones. Wouldn't it make your company a lot more credible if the key words "social responsibility" yielded a news story about your latest environmental initiative or a statement of company policy against sweatshop labor?

On the flip side, if there are controversial issues surrounding your company being discussed online or in the media, the search results on your own sites should reveal those conversations as well. If you use FAQ engines, update them constantly and keep them relevant by looking beyond your backyard to the tenor of conversation in the CGM environment.

Remember, transparency requires full disclosure. You're much better off telling your side of the story than trying to hide it.

4. Show *all* ratings and reviews.

Many consumers check ratings and reviews on a company's own Web site before they make a purchasing decision. After all, isn't it easier to visit a single company Web page than to pore through all the endless CGM on the Web? Smart companies like Best Buy and Circuit City, for example, import reviews—both positive and negative—to their own Web sites to aid consumers' decision-making process. (Of course, they must acknowledge the reviews' original sources.) And Dell, in the wake of the Jeff Jarvis disaster, even began to let consumers post reviews right on its Web site. On the surface, this may seem like negative marketing, but in fact it drives credibility. It's okay to let a consumer occasionally see a negative review about your brand on your own Web site; this transparency is more than compensated for by the trust and loyalty it conveys. In the same way, a waiter who occasionally wrinkles his nose at a menu item will have more credibility when he encourages you to try a different entrée; acknowledging criticism lends more credibility to the positive reviews.

5. DON'T PROMISE WHAT YOU CAN'T DELIVER!

A warning to marketers and advertisers: Don't push an ad claim beyond how the product or service actually performs. In today's world of CGM, companies should be particularly careful in the claims they make in their advertisements; exaggerating will only create or magnify credibility problems. Bloggers are superb scrutinizers of advertising claims, and they love to expose competing statements—a TV ad making one claim and a consumer testimonial starkly contradicting it, for example. In fact, in my analysis of over a million letters on PlanetFeedback, I found that the letters that generated the highest levels of negative word of mouth were about a major gap between brand promise and actual product performance.

Take cell phone service. Verizon has some very effective commercials that illustrate the size and strength of its wireless network. Yet Verizon has been said to routinely cripple the software that comes with its phones, and its ads never mention the two-year contract requirement or the cost of additional features. If you look carefully at the following brand-association map, which illustrates how consumers perceive advertising, you'll see why it is so important for companies today to advertise and market with transparency. Note how the term "false" sits closest to the term advertising—followed closely by the terms "misleading," "tactics," and "deceptive." In other words, consumers disproportionately associate advertising with lies or deceptive tactics.

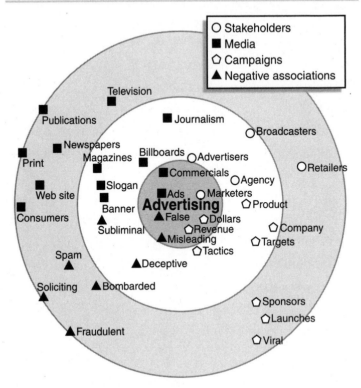

The Nielsen brand-association map on "Advertising"

Remember, your marketing and advertising is responsible for crafting the image of your company and products, and you will be held accountable for any claims that aren't 100 percent honest or accurate.

Nurture the Love Spot

While on a recent family vacation to my hometown of Pasadena, my wife and I took our twins on a stroll through the neighborhood, ultimately stopping at the local Peet's coffee shop. This particular Peet's had an unmistakable energy, enhanced by its diverse mix of local residents and brainy Caltech students, not to mention the sumptuous smell of Peet's dark roast mixing with a whiff of Noah's bagels from next door. Toward the end of a thoroughly enjoyable coffee experience, my wife and I noticed a prominent bulletin board covered with color photographs taken by Peet's patrons. A good ol' fashioned Polaroid instant camera was attached to the board by a strong cable.

Turns out, this was one of Peet's fortieth-anniversary events, designed to encourage patron participation. In our case, it clearly worked. Without skipping a beat, we proudly took a photo of our two little bambinos, wrote a "we love Peet's" note on it, and posted it at the very top of the bulletin board. (We took an extra photo as a souvenir, but please don't tell anyone!)

In the days that followed, we told all our friends and family about our contribution, encouraging them to drop by Peet's to check out our adorable photo—which most of them did, undoubtedly buying some coffee in the process. Peet's program was built on the very simple idea that customers who are encouraged to actively engage with brands they love will spread this love to others—and it worked.

I now officially dub this "the love spot," that critical moment of experience with a product or brand that makes positive feedback and word of mouth slide off your tongue like kids off a waterslide. The love spot is always well timed and often encouraged, but it is never—I repeat, never—forced.

A big reason so many companies fail at word-of-mouth marketing is that they don't know how to get their customers to discover the love spot. They push messages that have nothing to do with emotions or the actual customer experience. They should realize, like Peet's did, that consumers are engaged by a positive, authentic experience, and don't have to be seduced, enticed, or propped up with covert marketing or shills.

Turns out, the Peet's Family Album campaign has been a smashing success, collecting CGM of a nonelectronic variety at the moment of customer experience. Participation has been off the charts. As Peet's CMO, Christine Lansing, explained, "These photo boards have been a huge hit. Within a couple of days, they were filled with pictures, notes, drawings, etc. People *want* to be part of it . . . and they certainly have something to say!"

Let's contrast Peet's campaign with a recent effort by General Motors. GM also invited customer participation, encouraging consumers to create their own ads for the new Chevy Tahoe. As a copromotion with the reality television show *The Apprentice,* the campaign got plenty of blog and media attention. I even gave it big points on my blog for being bold, brave, and experimental.

But it didn't translate to a boom in customer loyalty, or sales. Why? Because GM completely missed the love spot. Since the contest wasn't targeted at Chevy Tahoe drivers, most of the ads were created by consumers who had never actually purchased, or even driven, the cars. As a result, the ads lacked the kind of genuine passion and enthusiasm that sends customers running to the car dealership.

How could GM have made this campaign more effective? Imagine if

- GM dealers gave all buyers cards asking (but not requiring) them to create their own ads after the first week of driving the vehicle.
- The GM Web site sent all recent buyers e-mails with a link to information about the campaign asking them write about their great experiences.
- GM sent e-mails about the ad campaign every time consumers provided online feedback or instructed call agents to tell consumers about the campaign when they called the company with positive feedback.

To GM's credit, its follow-up effort to involve consumers in the ad process was far more effective. This time, the company targeted college kids to create ads for cars that crossed over to the youth market (Aveo, Cobalt, HHR, and Equinox) and ended up with a very clever concept: the "Car Wash" ad, contributed by the University of Wisconsin-Milwaukee student Katie Crabb, which became a memorable thirty-second spot during the 2007 Super Bowl. GM may not have cornered the love spot, but by targeting college students who had relevant experience with the specific car brands, they got closer to the mark.

"WHERE ELSE CAN I FIND THE LOVE SPOT?"
The location of the love spot varies, but here are a few places to look.

- **In store:** Plenty of great experiences are nurtured at either the retail location or the point of purchase. The emotional connection has to be there for someone to actually make the purchase.
- **At the feedback moment:** True, some feedback is negative, but not all. There's a huge, untapped opportunity to turn consumer feedback into an engine for positive testimonials. For example, if a customer sends a rave about a product, that's a great time to encourage him or her to generate positive media and spread the brand loyalty to others.
- **On the Web site:** Web sites are increasingly extensions of product or brand experience. A user-friendly, consumer-oriented Web site can foster positive connections.

Every company has to pay attention to passionate, loyal users, because those brand ambassadors will jump through hoops for you. The future of marketing in an age of consumer control is getting those consumers to share their opinions and experiences with others. As Mark Jarvis, Dell's chief marketing officer, has been quoted as saying, "By listening to customer conversation, that is actually the most perfect form of marketing you could have."

Encourage Consumer Participation and Cocreation

Companies can drive positive word of mouth by inviting consumers to participate not only in creating the message, as exemplified by Peet's coffee, but also in creating the product or service itself. Not only does consumer involvement foster brand loyalty but the most involved consumers are among the best innovators for companies.

Ben & Jerry's was one of the first corporations to embrace the notion of user participation, long before all the Web 2.0 hoopla, by inviting customers to vote on new ice-cream flavors. And, the interactive features on its Web site—like the virtual tour of the ice-cream-making process (called "from Cow to Cone")—continue to foster enthusiasm and involvement.

Lego also has been at the forefront of cocreation; it encourages fans to design and develop new uses for the classic toy. Lego even set up extensive listening labs in which these highly engaged consumers serve almost like company employees in helping to come up with new designs. In fact, Lego's bestselling, breakthrough product Mindstorms was developed largely based on consumer input. By involving consumers in the product development process, the company boosted loyalty rates and positive buzz.

User involvement was Dell's secret to success in the mid-1990s, when Dell Direct, which empowered buyers to customize, configure, and buy Dell computers online, proved a big hit, generating sales of nearly $15 million a day. "Something powerful happens when consumers configure their own machines," said Norm Lehoullier, former president of Grey Interactive, the firm that helped develop the Dell Direct model. "Brand loyalty is nurtured by the process of allowing consumers to participate in the design and configuration of the end product. It created a higher 'value' equation."

Another successful user-participation model was M&M's breakthrough Global Color Vote initiative, in which nearly 10 million consumers voted for the new M&M's colors. Again, involvement strengthened consumers' emotional ties to the brand, boosting loyalty and, by extension, sales.

In my early days at Procter & Gamble, of the hundreds of online ad campaigns we tested, the most effective one by far was based on user participation. This is because content created by other consumers not only has an unusual, if somewhat raw, creative twist but also comes across as more authentic and trustworthy—and therefore credible—to other consumers. People believe—most often correctly—that fellow consumers who create ads do so out of genuine affection for the brand, not to satisfy a paid contract. However, whether consumer participation in advertising will remain effective is uncertain. If every company does it, or it starts to seem contrived, the credibility factor may diminish.

Integrate Your Online and Offline Message

In 2007, a Super Bowl ad cost $2.7 million for a thirty-second spot. The halftime show alone typically costs the sponsor $15 to $20 million. Yet in four years of carefully analyzing Super Bowl advertising, I found that the ads that reaped the highest rewards and attention before, during, and after the game were for brands with the best Web site strategies.

Marketers often talk about "online-offline integration" or "cross-platform synergy." But these aren't just buzzwords. In a world where almost every home has an Internet connection in every room and a growing number of us can watch television on our iPods, moble devices, and cell phones, more consumers than ever are toggling back and forth between the Internet and television. But even in the age of DVR and TiVo, advertisers can't afford to abandon the television ad completely. The solution? Complement and enhance your offline advertising through your Web site.

In the 2007 Super Bowl game, Doritos, FedEx, GM, and Budweiser all got the most out of their TV ad dollars by synchronizing their online and offline advertising. They not only posted their TV ads prominently on their Web sites but also added "extras" related to the ads, blogged about the ads on their company blogs, and flooded their brand and corporate Web sites with even more related content. The buzz these strategies generated was only amplified by the media coverage they received for their smart strategies and effective execution.

Another company that employed similar tactics with impressive results during the 2007 Super Bowl was Nationwide Insurance, with its memorable "Life Comes at You Fast" spot. Contrary to what some may think, this spot was *not* a success because it featured Britney Spears's ex, Kevin Federline; it succeeded because Nationwide mastered the principle of online-offline integration by doing the following:

- Priming the buzz by making the ad available well ahead of the game
- Aggressively promoting the ad on the Web site's home page
- Arming the Web site with "send-to-a-friend" links that allowed users to send the ad to others with the click of a mouse
- Providing "extras" like outtake interviews and behind-the-scenes material (the way DVDs do) related to the ad on the Web site

What was truly remarkable about Nationwide's campaign was that it created an unprecedented level of online commentary and buzz in a matter of weeks. In fact, it generated nearly as much indexed content on Google as all the Budweiser ads that have ever aired on the Super Bowl combined. Nationwide's vice president of advertising and brand management, Steven R. Schreibman, told *The New York Times* that the goal was for their commercial to "to have a life outside the Super Bowl." By using its trusted Web site as a vehicle for the ad, the company succeeded in driving a massive amount of online conversation and CGM. Plus, since the content of its Web site was consistent with its TV advertising, Nationwide's message was viewed as all the more authentic and credible.

But the Super Bowl is only one example of what's quickly becoming a trend in TV land. Attempts to synergize the television programming with the online content have increased dramatically since 2006, as TV networks have completely overhauled their Web sites and increased their online presence. In fact, every major TV or cable network has integrated user-generated content into its Web sites—from blogs, to wikis, to video-sharing—all with an eye toward drawing viewers to their TV programming by increasing online engagement. CBS, for example, even offers an editing studio that allows fans and aspiring filmmakers to create promotional videos that are then distributed on CBS.com and CBS Mobile. "Recognizing that short-form content is what our viewers want online, we're committed to bringing CBS fans short, easy to digest clips which they can take and mash up, rework, re-edit, and, no doubt, inspire us with their creativity," said Anthony Suiker, executive producer and creator of *CSI*, in a recent interview.

One thing is clear in these developments: The brand, company, or product Web site is absolutely indispensable in building loyalty and credibility around the production. In the next chapter, you'll learn even more about how to bolster credibility on every front via the company Web site.

Chapter 5

Postcards from the Welcome Mat: Credibility and Your Web Site

On April 1, 2007 (opening day of the baseball season), James Furdell logged on to ESPN.com to make some trades to his fantasy baseball team. However, much to his chagrin, he found his team roster stuck—it wouldn't let him make any cuts or pick up any new players. This was no April Fool's Day joke; something was very wrong with ESPN's online game. Furdell, a rabid fantasy baseball fan, was mad. So he vented his anger on his blog and on fantasy baseball message boards. By the end of the week, ESPN was flooded with complaints from other players who'd experienced similar frustration with the game's glitch.

Wisely, ESPN was quick to respond. Once it identified the problem in the software, it immediately set out to make repairs, sent players regular e-mails updating them on the progress, and promised free access to premium content to all fantasy players once the site was back up and running. And although some die-hard players like Furdell might not have gone back to ESPN for fantasy baseball the next season, the network's genuine efforts to respond to and remedy the problem were the smartest way to avoid alienating too many customers.[2]

Today, companies are increasingly using games and contests—like fantasy baseball—to drive people to their Web sites. Why? Because companies have realized that, because corporate Web sites are, by nature, opt-in, nonintrusive, and informational, they have the potential to broker considerable trust with consumers. In fact, a major study I helped conduct on trust and brand credibility found that company Web sites were among the most trusted advertising vehicles—more trusted than TV and radio ads, product placements, and online banner or search ads.

And in late 2007, Nielsen released a study revealing that consumers initially place extraordinarily more trust in brand Web sites than even customer testimonials, news stories, or other advertisements. When asked what source they would be most likely to consult when searching for information on the Internet about a product or brand, a whopping 55 percent of the nearly 70,000 consumers surveyed said they would first click on a company Web site or blog. But the sad fact is, most companies severely underleverage their Web sites. Even in today's online world, many simply don't realize how much a Web site can boost their business—if, as ESPN learned the hard way, that Web site is credible.

Think about the opportunities. As the first place consumers go to find information about your organization, brand, or product, your company Web site is in many ways the hub of your business. Millions of people visit corporate Web sites every day, and those numbers are growing with the overall growth of the Web. But *visiting* a Web site is a far cry from *talking* about a Web site. A company can always direct traffic or buy visits to its site, but this doesn't necessarily translate into positive buzz or CGM. Conversation needs to be earned. To get consumers talking, your company's site content must be useful, timely, sticky, inviting, and engaging—deserving of being shared or sent. Information must be easy to find, always relevant, and consistent with how the company has positioned itself. A well-managed Web site can generate a significant amount of consumer-generated media, and can be a huge driver of credibility.

Consumers who spread good or bad news about corporations are always looking for useful, actionable content. Corporations should know that people who create CGM tend to utilize the content on company Web sites to inform or confirm their own blog posts, product reviews, or other online commentary. If they hear something about a company, they have a strong proclivity to check out its Web site before they broadcast their opinion. And if that site is viewed as a trusted, credible resource, they will link to it on their blogs, in their e-mails, on their MySpace pages, or in instant-messaging conversations, and as a result, the Web site becomes an extension of the consumers' own networks. This consumer could be a Power Mom who wants to double-check the health claims about a baby food product before making a recommendation to her network of fellow parents. Or it could be a Gadget Guy who needs all the facts and figures about the newest model of the MacBook before he renders a final judgment. It could be a Techno Teen linking all his friends to the best site for fantasy baseball. Or it could even be a Radical Flamethrower who wants to compare a company's claims with what he's read on the Web, simply for the fun of catching that company in a lie. In a way, these links provide social currency for companies; if your company Web site is credible, CGM influencers will spread this credibility far and wide.

You can build credibility into your Web site using the same core drivers that build credibility into other aspects of your business. Corporate sites can build trust and authenticity by serving as authoritative and dependable sources of information about all dimensions of the company and its products, and they are often the best means for tuning in to feedback and participating in useful and meaningful dialogue. Here are some tips to help you give your Web site a credibility makeover.

Make Your Web Site The Authority

A Web site needs to act like a trusted expert who is always there to serve needs, answer questions, provide directions, and offer advice.

At Procter & Gamble, we realized the value of building expert, informative Web sites early on, when we kicked off a site called Beinggirl.com. This site, sponsored by the Always and Tampax brands, offered advice from medical experts like Dr.

Iris Prager, who was available to answer questions from pre-teen girls on intimate topics. By providing professional, easy-to-understand answers to questions about their bodies that many girls were too shy or embarrassed to ask their friends or parents, Beinggirl.com established itself as *the* authority on those sensitive topics. And as a result, Always and Tampax enjoyed huge gains in credibility and in brand loyalty among their target consumers.

You can even create an expert Web site while having a little fun with your product. For example, Tide established its Web site as the authority on getting out stains by launching the "Stain Detective" application, an interactive feature that answered consumers' questions about how to get out their toughest stains. This was not just a fun feature; it actually became a very useful resource for stain-prone consumers, and it helped Tide establish itself as the authority in the product category—a reputation that spread virally through CGM.

However, if your Web site isn't viewed as authoritative, consumers will go elsewhere for information, and your credibility—not to mention your Web site traffic—will take a huge hit. During the 2007 pet food recall crisis, it was shocking how few consumers actually went to the major manufacturers' Web sites for information. When consumers talked about the recall, few referenced the Purina or Iams or Menu Foods sites as sources of trusted or authoritative content. That was because those Web sites provided only the most basic information: the names of the brands or products implicated in the recall. Even as the story exploded across the headlines and the blogosphere, these company sites remained static, failing to respond to breaking information about the cause of the contamination, the offending ingredients, and the origins of the tainted foods.

Meanwhile, consumer-generated Web sites, like Petconnection.com and Itchmo.com, proactively contacted manufacturers for information and then sent instant e-mail alerts notifying their subscribers about breaking recall news—scooping even the mainstream media. They also solicited and published tips from readers about what to do for a pet that got sick from the tainted food or what brands were the safest substitutes for the recalled products. When the press identified melamine as being responsible for the contamination, these sites immediately posted links to more detailed information about the chemical. Both Itchmo.com and Petconnection.com provided live podcasts of the first congressional hearing on the incident. In the end, these sites became the new experts—far more authoritative than the corporate sites—on pet food safety, and they received nearly twenty times as much CGM as all the pet food manufacturer Web sites combined.

Design Your Web Site to Be a Listening Platform

Instinctively, consumers assume a company's Web site is a listening post, but it's up to the company to fulfill that assumption. Because more consumers treat Web sites as first points of entry for so-called feedback moments, managers must use their Web sites as the first tools with which they respond to or engage with consumers.

Believe it or not, the design of your company's Web site has a big effect on how effective a listening platform it can be. It's common sense that the easier it is for consumers to find the portion of the site that solicits feedback, the more likely they will be to utilize it. On this front, organizations are all over the map. Brands like Geico and Gerber splash inviting "talk to us" buttons in prominent places on their Web sites, whereas McDonald's requires a scavenger hunt to find its unfriendly feedback forms. Your company Web site should be designed with this in mind. Make sure that every page—not just the home page—links to the feedback forms, and make sure the forms themselves are user-friendly and inviting.

There's another obvious reason to use your corporate Web site as a tool for active listening: Web sites sit on servers, and servers record everything—from clicks and page views to downloads and search queries. This is powerful intelligence corporations can harvest in real time to inform business strategy. And, as I described in Chapter 3, the tools to analyze such online behavior have gotten much more precise, revealing, and easy to use. For example, I use FeedBurner, now owned by Google, to tell me with razor-sharp precision how many folks are subscribing to my personal blog, which articles or posts they read, and how traffic grows or decreases over a set period. Knowing what pages on your company site are getting the most traffic and eyeballs, what posts on your company blog are getting the most commentary, or what searches are being performed most often can—and should—inform serious decision making across your organization.

The dramatic improvement in content-management tools can lend insight into not only what issues consumers are talking about but also which of your online initiatives or services are working. If your online reservation system, for example, is getting less and less traffic, that may be a clue that it's time to revamp the interface or upgrade the software. Listening to the digital trail people leave on your company Web site is one of the best ways to ensure that you are meeting the most relevant needs of your consumers.

So think about your corporate Web site as a huge, highly measurable, listening sensor, and make sure to design it for optimal use.

Embrace and Incorporate CGM

One of the best ways to broker trust with consumers is to include them in the conversation. In a 2004 Forrester study I helped put together, and in a subsequent 2007 Nielsen Global Trust study, "recommendations from other consumers" was rated higher for trust than any other form of communication, and interestingly, this is true across the globe, from Latin America to Europe to the Middle East. The fact of the matter is, consumers will always trust the word of other consumers over the word of companies or marketers, because consumers are perceived as more objective and authentic. Luckily, thanks to all the new participatory Web 2.0 technologies, consumers can be part of the conversation right on your company Web site. Inviting and incorporating CGM on your Web site is a great way to foster trust and drive credibility.

In July 2007, even the giant retailer Wal-Mart woke up to the realities of today's consumer-driven world, when it announced that it would be allowing consumers to rate and review products on the company site. As *Advertising Age* magazine put it, "The road to online retail dominance, Wal-Mart is finally figuring out, is paved with customer content."[3]

Circuit City, too, recently began inviting consumers to post product reviews alongside its product descriptions. At first, Circuit City executives were extremely reluctant to give this innovation the green light, fearing that negative reviews would drag down product sales. But they ultimately realized that including consumers in the conversation would lend more credibility to their site as a shopping destination.

Their leap of faith paid off. Far from pulling down sales, the user-generated product reviews were viewed as more trustworthy and authentic because they were written by other consumers, not shills or advertisers or marketers. Moreover, these candid reviews gave prospective buyers objective and important information right at the point of sale, which helped them make purchasing decisions with which they were ultimately more satisfied. Circuit City finally realized that consumers research and comparison-shop before they buy, and that they place a real value on the candid, sometimes critical, opinions of others. In fact, the *Ad Age* article referred to above reported a recent study which found that 75 percent of shoppers say it's extremely or very important to read customer reviews before making a purchase, and that 80 percent of shoppers have more trust in brands that feature reviews. By opting to embrace CGM in the form of product reviews on their company sites, Circuit City and Wal-Mart drove not only trust and credibility but also better online sales.

Start a Corporate Blog

Creating a company or product blog, if properly executed, is another fantastic way to establish trust with consumers. Because they are so simple, convenient, and low cost (in fact, most blogs are free and require no knowledge of programming language), blogs are rapidly becoming one of the most popular communications vehicles around. But beyond their role as personal diaries and gossipy news journals, blogs can serve as extraordinarily powerful corporate communications tools; if a company blog is open, honest, authentic, transparent, and in touch with prevailing trends, it can greatly enhance both the experience and the credibility of the corporate Web site.

Corporate blogs should make full use of available Web 2.0 tools up to and including podcasts, videocasts, and site measurement tools. The most credible corporate blogs include open privacy statements, clear definitions of acceptable user behavior (including commenting guidelines), and a steady stream of interesting and vibrant content. If content is just a stale rehash of corporate press releases or company news sanitized to the point that no life remains, bored readers will shy away. However, a corporate blog that is too free-swinging and "out there" runs the risk of being seen as unfocused. Corporate blogs must walk a fine line between being interesting and informative and not going too far off message.

General Motors was one of the first out of the gate, with its FastLane blog, which succeeded in giving the company a brand-new face. On FastLane, a wide variety of GM execs and workers, up to and including Vice Chairman Bob Lutz, discuss topics like the design and development of current and future car models, explain GM's policies on salient issues like fuel economy and gas prices, offer behind-the-scenes accounts of recent car shows or expos, and respond to consumers' questions and comments. Their commentary is refreshingly open and candid; in fact, in a recent post about the concept for a new electrically driven vehicle, the Chevrolet Volt, Lutz wrote: "We plan to keep everyone up to speed on our progress and to discuss openly and transparently the technological, engineering and design hurdles we face."

Despite all its woes, Dell, too, has learned the value of using a blog to promote transparency. In July 2006, Dell launched Direct2Dell.com, a blog that was said to "give the company a frank and credible human voice." While most brand Web sites barely mention problems with their products, the Dell corporate blog has well over a dozen entries about recalls. This fact got widespread attention, ultimately generating more comments per blog post than any major corporation. By using the corporate blog to address issues that ordinarily would be kept under the covers, Dell took the first few steps in restoring its damaged reputation in the wake of the Jeff Jarvis scandal. And it worked. So much so, in fact, that in just a year after its launch, customer satisfaction with the Dell brand shot up from 58 percent to 74 percent. Plus, thanks to the blog, when you search for "Dell" on Google, some of the anti-Dell results have been replaced with more positive ones.

Another example of a company that effectively uses a blog to express its corporate values, focus, and mission in a very real and transparent manner is Stonyfield Farm, maker of popular yogurts and other dairy-based products. Written by one of the farmers who supplies the milk that goes into Stonyfield Farm products, The Bovine Bugle blog offers visitors an informative and authentic perspective on sustainable agriculture and organic farming. And since parents, naturally, are interested in the health benefits of Stonyfield Farm products, the company created a separate blog for them to "meet up, rant, offer and seek advice, or just tell us their trials and triumphs."

The corporate blog can also be used to help strengthen emotional ties to your company or brand. Southwest Airlines for example, encourages employees to blog not only about corporate matters but about their personal lives, too. A recent and quite moving post, for example, described an employee's trip on Southwest to the wedding of a friend she hadn't seen in years. Other entries include a detailed trip report by a flight attendant, which gave readers great insights into the lengths employees go to when doing their jobs. Southwest's corporate blog is an excellent reflection of the airline's core values and way of doing business. Passengers may have been packed in like sardines on the last Southwest flight I took, but these folks are the masters of making it all tolerable and enjoyable (on what other airline would the captain announce, "Group hug!" and lead passengers in a round of the old camp song "Kumbaya"?)—and their blog shows it.

As you can see, corporate blogs do not have to be cookie cutter in their approach. You can use blogging tools to create fun interactive features or to flaunt information about upcoming events or promotions. Netflix, for example, uses its public calendar feature to announce when the hot new releases are coming out. Identify the purpose of the blog first, then brainstorm creative ideas for how you can fulfill that purpose. Finally, make sure your content is continually fresh, engaging, and relevant to the changing needs of consumers. Think of your corporate blog as a vehicle for building loyalty and celebrating your company and your brand.

Nurture Community

Another great way companies can grow consumer trust and loyalty through their Web sites is by creating online communities and social networks. This doesn't mean simply starting a company page on Facebook or MySpace (although that, too, can be an effective marketing strategy), but it means actually creating and building a community on your company's own site. This is very effective for several reasons. First, since social networks and online communities are nonhierarchical, they foster authentic, genuine dialogues in which consumers and companies have equal voices. Remember, in our online world, businesses are no longer in control; today, relationships between companies and consumers must be built on two-way communication and mutual respect. Second, inviting consumers to join their networks gives companies a clear vantage point from which to observe, and even participate in, honest, real-time, consumer-consumer discussions. And finally, social networks and online communities are fun and organic platforms for consumer participation and involvement, which, as I've mentioned, fosters loyalty and strengthens emotional ties.

The financial services company Intuit has made its Web site more conversational—and hence more useful—through online communities. In the last several years, Intuit has hosted over four major communities comprising over 150,000 members. Among them, JumpUp is a popular community for entrepreneurs and aspiring business owners that allows members to set up profiles similar to those on MySpace or other social networking sites and share advice and information with members in similar industries or locations.

"Our goal is to build an infrastructure to help small business owners get their questions answered by other users," explained Intuit's Scott Wilder. "Our community Web site is a tremendous way to learn about what small businesses need." In other words, this niche community not only helps users share information but also provides Intuit with valuable market research. In many respects, Intuit's focus on community is an extension of its founder, Scott Cook's "follow-me-home" initiative. Way back in the early days of the company, Cook asked product managers to quite literally follow consumers home (with their permission, of course) and observe how they used Intuit products. Similarly, by listening to the flow of conversation and feedback on its social networks, Intuit obtains firsthand observations that help the company improve its products.

Nike, too, has strengthened its relationships with its consumers by creating online social networks. And because these online communities are centered on specific sports rather than products, they come across as more genuine and authentic—and foster more enthusiasm because they tap into fans' love of their favorite game. On the online running community, Nike+, for example, running enthusiasts from all over the world can challenge one another to races, map runs, swap music recommendations, and even download one another's favorite running mixes. And this has boosted not just consumer involvement but also sales; *BusinessWeek* magazine reports that, according to Nike's vice president of global brand management, 40 percent of the people who join the Nike+ community end up becoming Nike wearers.[4]

Another example of a company that has built up a following on a social network is Turner Broadcasting, which recently launched a network called SuperDeluxe.com. Through this community, fans can post original video clips and shorts, share facts about featured artists, and chat about their favorite programming. The site has helped strengthen ties with existing viewers and attract new ones. After all, what could be more credible than an environment where product enthusiasts engage in open, honest, and authentic conversations with one another—and watch funny videos of rapping Muppets in the process?

Bottom line: A credible corporate Web site will reap outsize rewards in CGM. So no matter what industry your company is in, getting your Web site strategy on track should be a high priority and a no-brainer.

Chapter 6

This Company May Be Monitored for Quality Purposes: Credibility in Your Product

I knew companies were entering a brave new world when Procter & Gamble introduced its promising new olestra product Olean, a no-calorie oil that was thirty years in the making. But despite all the buzz, and anticipation over the exciting new product, P&G had a serious problem: Olean was being hammered by activist groups like the Center for Science in the Public Interest (CSPI), who claimed it had unsafe, not to mention unpleasant, side effects like abdominal cramping and diarrhea, or what the Food and Drug Administration labeled as "loose stool."

Unfortunately for P&G, CSPI posted this damaging information on its Web site, then circulated it to health advocacy groups and consumers throughout the Web. Internet communities soon seized on and satirized the term *anal leakage*, and the mainstream media played up CSPI's side of the story. And while P&G complied with the FDA's labeling requirements, did its best to be transparent about documented problems with Olean/olestra consumption, and spent a great deal of time responding to almost relentless CSPI claims, the bottom line was that Olean failed to live up to consumers' expectations on a number of other fronts as well, most notably its taste was unappealing and its price was too high. As a result, within roughly three years, sales fell sharply, from $400 to $200 million.

By contrast, when Procter & Gamble launched Febreze as a way to reduce or eliminate odors (unlike air fresheners, Febreze is a spray-on odor remover that can be used for pets, in cars, and in places other than the home), it was considered a breakthrough product. As a result, it generated many conversations online—mostly among parents and homemakers who had tried or were curious to try the new product. At first, this online chatter helped to build momentum and positive attention for the brand. But soon, that same network began to fuel a number of unfounded rumors, such as the allegation that Febreze is toxic for pets. Despite all the negative publicity, Febreze maintained its credibility as a reliable product because P&G's forthright and transparent communications strategy addressed the misinformation and held sway over the negative buzz.

Today, Febreze remains one of the company's most successful products, with multiple spin-off products. Of course, one of the other reasons that Febreze successfully managed the problem was that the rumors regarding its product were untrue, as opposed to the concerns about Olean, which were very real.

In all my years studying companies and brands, one truth

has consistently endured: Great brands and great products reap the richest CGM benefits. This may seem obvious, but if you don't get it right, consumers not only won't buy your stuff but will skewer you with CGM as well. The rule of product performance applies to all categories, from autos and electronics to everyday household items, like soap or diapers. If the product or service underperforms, CGM creators will not hesitate to make it known. Conversely, great products can inspire incredible amounts of free advertising and publicity.

In fact, the 2007 Nielsen study mentioned earlier, drawn from nearly 70,000 consumer panels, found that "product experience" is the number one motivator of CGM creation; nearly 55 percent of consumers determined to be active "speakers"—or creators of CGM—noted that liking a product was the top motivator for "posting content to a Web site, blog, or message board."

Intuitively, this makes sense. Why would consumers commit to a brand that didn't work? And if you have a great brand or product, consumers will *want* to recommend it to other consumers. The brand experience then provides a credible and genuine context for dialogue between consumers. This is one of the reasons why, despite its detractors, the Starbucks brand continues to be credible—people simply like the coffee.

Many companies have gained a competitive advantage thanks to attentive advocates of their products. Early sales of Sony PlayStation skyrocketed after highly detailed reviews by consumers appeared online. Lexus sales have benefited because buyers of these luxury cars are also unusually effusive in their commentary on message boards and online forums. Even some health-care companies have reaped benefits from patients blogging about good experiences with their products and services.

Of course, this environment can be equally punishing to products that have shortcomings, as the consumers who write the reviews tend to be the most attentive and committed to ferreting out flaws. Moreover, disgruntled customers are often the most opinionated and most motivated to warn others.

Take for example, Charlene Blake, who raised a stink over Toyota engine oil sludge and started a Toyota car owners' petition called "Toyota Owners Unite for Resolution." Although it's unclear how many other Toyota owners have gotten behind her effort, Blake gained an almost ubiquitous presence across key auto forums and blogs, and she's unusually detailed in her comments about Toyota product quality.

Is Blake typical? Probably not. Does she have disproportionate influence on the Internet? If Google search results are any indication, the answer is a big yes. Over 50,000 results show up for the search string "Charlene Blake and Toyota."

In a PlanetFeedback survey, nearly 84 percent of consumers said that product performance was most important to a company's credibility. As we like to say, if the product fails, the consumer wails, and expresses pain to others. If the product soars, the consumer roars—loudly and proudly.

That's why creating a high-quality product that consumers can trust from the very beginning is so fundamentally important in nurturing and protecting credibility. Here's how.

Make Sure Your Products Live Up to Their Promise

Ultimately, a company's core promise is its product. And in this age of consumer control, companies need to work extra hard to deliver on that promise, because if your product doesn't affirm the claims that your company is making about it, the world will find out.

Apple is one company that enjoys incredibly high levels of credibility because its products do what they claim to . . . and then some. If you read the digital trail of consumer comments, you'll find that Apple products are consistently touted for their high performance, creative output, sleek designs, and more. The result is extraordinarily high levels of brand loyalty and evangelism. A 2005 Forrester Research Technology Brand Scorecard found that Apple rated highest in brand trust among 15,000 respondents, and in 2007, the Reputation Institute ranked Apple among the highest brands in loyalty and customer appreciation. But you probably didn't need a study to tell you that—just think of how many people you've seen using a Mac or listening to an iPod in the past week.

What's unique about Apple products is that they are as much about experience as about technology. In a 2006 survey, Apple scored as being the best brand to buy directly from the manufacturer and the best walk-in store. With its sleek interior design, high-tech gadgets on display, and computer wizard–like staff, the experience of the Apple Store is truly impressive. And when consumers describe this experience, they are complimenting not just a store but Apple's broader product. On the heels of Apple's tremendous success at building in-store experiences into its products, other major electronics players—from Sony to Samsung—are now rethinking their approach to their retail environment.

As far as your company's credibility is concerned, one thing is absolute: If a product doesn't do what it is supposed to do, no fancy marketing or public relations spin can make up for it. Your products need to work, and ideally have a wow factor. If you review the diverse tapestry of online comments about any product, you'll see that its basic efficacy—or lack thereof—is the bedrock of the CGM landscape.

Be 100 Percent Transparent About Everything That Goes into Your Product

In 2007, Ralph Nader's nonprofit advocacy group, Public Citizen, posted several videos on YouTube highlighting some of the dangers of the new birth control substance, desogestrel, which, according to Public Citizen, could double the risk of blood clots. Of course, many medications have possible side effects, however, Organon, the maker of the drug, made a big mistake by failing to disclose this potential risk in its advertising and on its Web site. This omission invited intense scrutiny and exposure from Public Citizen and other advocacy groups, and ignited a panic among fertile women nation-wide. By failing to be transparent about the risks, Organon let Public Citizen control the story.

If you type "desogestrel" into Wikipedia, you'll see a defi-nition and source material that gives disproportionate cover-age to Public Citizen's findings. In fact, the only link in the "References" section is to the Public Citizen petition docu-ment. Moreover, if you type the name of this product into Google, a host of negative entries show up, including those precipitated by Public Citizen. If Organon had been more open to begin with, it could have addressed and alleviated consumers' concerns, but because the company was secre-tive, consumers could only wonder what other risks it was hiding.

Pet food manufacturers across North America recently learned a similar lesson about transparency and their prod-ucts. In March 2007, after hundreds of pets became ill or died from a mysterious pet food contaminant, major manu-facturers like the Canada-based Menu Foods and Procter & Gamble's Iams came under attack and were forced to pull hundreds of products off the shelves. But it didn't end there. When it was discovered that the deaths were caused by gluten imported from China, where factories were mixing the in-dustrial chemical melamine into many of the food and feed additive products routinely imported into the United States and Canada, the anxiety over pet food erupted into a wide-spread panic about the safety of human food products (many of which are imported from the very same factories in

China). As the story played out across the headlines—both online and offline—over several months, more and more food suppliers were exposed for importing tainted goods, and a broader scandal spread across the Web like wildfire.

This incident has intensified the pressure on suppliers (Menu Foods lost over $45 million in hundreds of recalled products and now faces numerous class-action suits) to be more transparent about their products and where they come from. Before the incident, most buyers of brands like Iams and Purina assumed that the ingredients in these products came from safe, federally regulated sources, and they were shocked to find out this was not the case (in fact, only 1 percent of imported food products are actually examined by FDA inspectors). In the wake of this scandal, food products are being put under a very public microscope, and companies that fail to fully and openly disclose supplier information on their packaging are being slammed by CGM.

Whether your company sells pet food, designs software, or provides financial services, it is critical to be 100 percent transparent not only about your end product but also about everything that goes into making it. This means disclosing the origins of all materials, ingredients, or parts; identifying all manufacturers and suppliers; and being open about all labor policies and practices in every factory, plant, retail space, or office.

Nike has learned, the hard way, the importance of being transparent about everything that goes into making its popular athletic shoes and clothing. Indeed, for years Nike's credibility has been severely challenged by reports that it exploits sweatshop labor. While Nike has always enjoyed strong sales, pervasive concern, skepticism, and criticism about its lack of social responsibility has clearly hurt the company. Analysis of CGM for the brand found that once stories about Nike's irresponsible labor practices hit the Internet, they quickly multiplied, as Nike critics found more platforms and audiences. As a result, when consumers (or reporters) typed "Nike" into Google, reminders of the company's poor practices would inevitably appear at the top of the search results.

But rather than trying to hide information from the public, Nike took a risk and addressed the problem head-on by publishing all its supplier information on the Web. The logic was that with this information freely available, consumers would see that Nike was open about practices and was taking steps to be more socially responsible. This decision went a long way toward restoring Nike's credibility—and stemming the tide of negative CGM about the corporation.

Accept Responsibility for Your Product's Flaws

But merely being open about your product is not enough. In the event that your product fails or is flawed, it is up to you to respond. In today's consumer-driven world, there is no credibility without accountability, period.

Take the Thomas the Tank Engine incident. In a pattern of events similar to the pet food scandal, when it was discovered that Chinese factories were using toxic lead paint on this popular toy, its manufacturer, RC2, voluntarily recalled 1.5 million toys and parts. However, this response was not nearly enough to curtail the flood of negative CGM that soon enveloped the brand. With the exception of a brief press release, RC2 failed to respond to the letters, calls, and complaints of concerned parents nationwide, refused all interview requests, and offered only the vaguest information about why it had taken the company so long to discover the safety hazard.

Furthermore, much to the ire of its already angry customers, RC2 refused to cover the cost of shipping the recalled toys back to the factory; although eventually the company relented, under pressure, this too-little-too-late concession didn't do much to win back public favor. Thanks to RC2's mishandling of the situation, a product that was once regarded as a wholesome, harmless, even educational toy, is now viewed with suspicion and distrust.

However, when Mattel found itself in the middle of a disturbingly similar recall scandal in September 2006, it weathered the storm far better. In what seemed a bit like déjà vu, when this toy-making giant was forced to recall 19 million lead-paint-covered toys (the biggest recall in company history), CEO Robert A. Eckert immediately issued a very public video apology and vowed to take immediate steps to prevent dangerous toys from ever reaching consumers again. Mattel then implemented a three-check system—from that point forward they would test all paint for lead, conduct unannounced spot-checks and inspections at every stage of the manufacturing process, and test every production run of finished toys—and posted this information and more on its Web site. All in all, Mattel went out of its way to show consumers that the safety of children was its number one priority—and many consumers believed them.

What's particularly notable about Mattel's management of the crisis is that the company effectively borrowed from CGM tactics to get its point across. As YouTube, and even television, has made so clear, video is perhaps the most emotionally engaging medium. Therefore, by stepping up to the camera and using video format to quickly communicate with concerned customers about the crisis, Eckert came across as more authentic and credible than he would have if he had addressed the issues through a written statement.

The point is, today, companies need to listen to the concerns of their customers (particularly when the concerns have to do with the safety of pets or young children) and hold themselves accountable for anything that has gone wrong. Remember, your company's reputation hinges on what people think of your products, so if your products aren't credible, you're in serious trouble.

Chapter 7

No Place to Hide: Credibility and the CEO

n July 2007, Whole Foods Market's CEO, John Mackey, was publicly outed for posting over one thousand comments, most of which were attacks on a rival organic food retailer, on a Yahoo! bulletin board under a false identity. When the story broke, consumers were outraged. How, people asked, could an executive of *Whole Foods,* so committed to causes as authentic as organic farming, sustainable living, and social responsibility, have behaved so inauthentically? The negative buzz resounded all over the Web as well as the mainstream media, and the fallout was felt among the hundreds of thousands of employees across the company's 196 stores—all thanks to the dishonest behavior of a single executive.

An organization's chief executive is its most visible spokesperson. The CEO is ultimately the figure held accountable for a company's products or performance, so what he or she says, claims, or promises simply must hold true. If consumers uncover data or evidence that contradicts what the CEO is saying, there will be a huge backlash of negative consumer-generated media—and it will affect everyone in the organization.

Increasingly, today's CEO is accountable for both the corporate party line and the unofficial story. As we've seen, social media sites, user-generated videos, and blogs spread unofficial information about companies, and consumers absorb and internalize such information just as much as, if not more than, they do the information that comes from the company itself. What's more, media writers now rely on CGM sources to inform them about companies or products, and they spread this information through mainstream print, TV, or radio outlets.

Corporate CEOs have to confront this fundamental new reality. The CEO is crucial to the company's image, yet the CEO's storytelling is often contradicted or compromised by other information. A CEO may parade a customer satisfaction study or service award to demonstrate the company's focus on customer loyalty, for example, while a blogger reveals a trove of consumer commentary suggesting precisely the opposite. Or the CEO might assert the company's commitment to green technologies while a video on YouTube captures a company truck dumping nonbiodegradable waste into a landfill. Or the CEO might say employees are happy and motivated, while an employee's public blog suggests that morale is at a low and that the entire enterprise is a shambles.

Now, thanks to CGM, questions about companies are bubbling to the surface faster than ever before, creating new challenges and frustrations for CEOs in trying to control and shape their companies' messaging. At Nielsen, we often see incidents in which a CEO or senior executive was caught off guard by a zinger question that stemmed from a highly revealing online post or blog entry. Today, the CEO simply cannot afford to be out of step with the external commentary.

The Credibility Quadrant

The Credibility Quadrant is a tool to help executives better understand the impacts that decisions and investments throughout the organization have on CGM. The chart maps marketing strategies according to how credible and accepted they are in the eyes of consumers, as well as the degree of control companies have over their content.

Companies that invest resources in strategies in the upper-right quadrant are rewarded with the most favorable consumer-generated media. These are the tactics and strategies that have high credibility and over which the company has a high level of control. You can readily see that they include business fundamentals and processes such as product quality, customer service, and employee behavior, rather than buzz-building tactics over which the company has far less control. This is why it is important for companies to be accountable to consumers in each and every activity.

Of course, the Credibility Quadrant is not a one-size-fits-all model. It may look quite different applied in various industries. In electronics, consumer affairs or tech support may have more of an impact on credibility. In household goods or health-care products, television advertising matters more. As a CEO, you must understand the degree to which every aspect of your business strategies and marketing tactics influences credibility.

USING THE CREDIBILITY QUADRANT

So what do I recommend to CEOs? The first step is to look at the Credibility Quadrant and ask the following questions:

- What drives the conversation, hence reputation, about my corporation?

The Credibility Quadrant

	Brand Communities		Brand Web sites
	Ratings/Reviews	Feedback/Listening	Contact Us
Boards, Forums	E-mail–opt-in		Paid Search
Consumer Blogs		Human Touch	Brand Search
Cocreation Extreme		Brand/Corp Blogs	RSS
	Organic Search	On-Demand Video	
		Product Quality	Cocreation Limited

High Consumer Acceptance

	Direct Mail	Print Ads
		TV Advertising
		Ads Before Movies
	E-mail Spam	
Stealth Marketing	Shilling	Splog	Phone Solicitation

Low Consumer Acceptance

Low Company/ Brand Control   **High Company/ Brand Control**

- What ways to shape the flow and tenor of CGM are within my control?
- Which departments or divisions of my company are implicated in the CGM?
- Which policies, priorities, or decisions are implicated in the CGM?
- To what extent does the conversation challenge, rebut, or reinforce my message to consumers?
- What specific strategies and business processes should be initiated to create long-term credibility?

The CEO may be the only person who can answer these questions *and* coordinate integration among various arms of the organization, like consumer affairs and marketing, or IT and online sales. As a result, it often falls upon the CEO to address the issues that sit in the upper-right box of the quadrant. But in order to do so, executives need to be tapped into the feedback pipeline.

The CEO and the Feedback Pipeline

The CEO needs to determine the company's overall philosophy for responding to feedback from consumers. This involves setting the stage for how the listening process will adapt to the newer, more viral forms of expression, like video, audio, or multimedia channels. Can the feedback pipeline be used as an entry point to shape a fundamentally new marketing model? Does it provide constructive information about improving efficiency and operations? Does it illuminate new sources of value for the corporation? The CEO should be committed to making sure the company can safely answer yes to all these questions.

While ultimately the responsibility for overseeing a company's CGM (either directly or by hiring an outside firm) should fall to the CEO, there is no reason why he or she can't delegate CGM monitoring duties to a trusted associate. At Toyota, for example, there is an executive position called Corporate Manager of Consumer Generated Media (held by Bruce Ertmann). In an age when keeping a finger on the pulse of CGM is so important, such organizational roles should become commonplace.

A strong commitment to listening and responsiveness should come straight from the CEO and be at the core of the company mission statement. Executives should recognize the importance of measuring CGM and ensure that all groups within the organization respond to and apply the data as appropriate. When Toyota Motor Sales, for example, hired Nielsen to analyze CGM for the engineering group, senior executives soon learned that the information was equally useful to other divisions, including PR, marketing, advertising, and external relations. In cases like these, it is the responsibility of the CEO to make sure this information reaches all relevant divisions.

CEOs Adopting the Consumer Megaphone

Just as marketers have mirrored consumer behavior by starting company blogs similar to consumer blogs, CEOs can draw on consumers' communications techniques. Corporate leaders have also taken advantage of such social networking sites as Facebook, LinkedIn, and Ecademy to connect with and engage peers and others. These sites not only generate consumer enthusiasm and involvement but also serve as incubators of ideas shared between the like-minded.

Marriott International's chairman, Bill Marriott, for example, not only writes his company's corporate blog but even takes the time to provide an audio version of his posts. His blog is refreshingly void of corporate speak and offers behind-the-scenes glimpses of the company. Often, news about companies appears first in the mainstream media and then finds its way to the blog; for Marriott, this isn't the case. An announcement of Marriott Hotels's commitment to build twenty Nickelodeon by Marriott hotels worldwide, for example, appeared on Bill Marriott's corporate blog the very same day it hit the rest of the media.

Or take David Neeleman, the former CEO of JetBlue Airways, one of the first CEOs of a major company to use a consumer-generated multimedia platform to speak to customers. Faced with a crisis of unparalleled proportions when thousands of customers were left on the runway for over six hours during a snowstorm, Neeleman recorded a very public apology and posted it on YouTube. While many ad agencies struggle to get even 10,000 views of a commercial on YouTube, Neeleman's announcement drew over 300,000 views in a matter of days, garnered a four-star rating, and was picked up and broadcast in mainstream media. Consumers soon flooded YouTube with supportive comments. People accepted Neeleman's apology because it was authentic and responsive, and conveyed a sense of accountability. Not only was JetBlue, he said, horrified by what had happened but, in keeping with its historic commitment to making things right, the company would compensate monetarily those who were inconvenienced. In addition, JetBlue announced the first ever "Passenger Bill of Rights," which went miles beyond fluff to holding the firm fully accountable for future screwups. This allowed JetBlue to overcome the crisis and win back credibility. And although Neeleman did, several months later, step down as CEO, his parting was voluntary and amicable—he wasn't forced out by shareholders angry over the incident.

Jonathan Schwartz, CEO of Sun Microsystems, wins point in credibility because he perfectly embodies the spirit of the consumer blogger. His blog entries are interesting and engaging, and reflect his genuine enthusiasm for what Sun is doing. Says the noted blog expert and author Debbie Weil, "Schwartz manages to be informal and conversational while also substantive and sometimes even revealing. It's a delicate balance. It's easy to be breezy when you're not really saying anything. But when you're talking about earnings forecasts or a shift in strategy, it's more difficult. Plus he's a superb writer."

Richard Edelman of the communications firm Edelman, who has been blogging for over three years, is another corporate blogger who is viewed as credible because he blogs like a consumer. He speaks in his own authentic voice, and much of what he writes comes from firsthand experience. At times, his blog reads like a travel and event diary, providing readers with a unique window into his daily itinerary.

David Brain, the CEO of Edelman Europe, is equally passionate about blogging. Drawing from the success formulas of consumer video bloggers, Brain created a blog called Sixtysecondview, on which he simply captures one-minute video blurbs from various folks he meets on the road, at work, and beyond. At first interviews were with "figures from business, media, government and NGOs on topics of the moment with a public relations or public affairs flavour," but he's expanded into other topics of interest to his audience.

Online video in a corporate blog can be used to great effect in managing, containing, or even reversing a crisis or the spread of rumors. If properly and credibly executed, video can drive or reinforce deeper emotional connections as well as convey greater authenticity and sincerity when times are tough. If the content or gesture doesn't appear real or authentic, you won't get anywhere, but if you do have something important to say, clarify, or defend, go for video—the highest-return vehicle.

At the height of Mattel's 2006 toy recall, for example, an online video featuring CEO Robert Eckert reaching out to calm public and parental anxiety was right on the mark. By showing the highest figure in the organization connecting emotionally and demonstrating empathy, this video was a smart first step in winning back consumer trust.

Companies should aggressively think about how to leverage interactive capabilities and platforms, especially video, to drive deeper emotional connections and trust with consumers. Here are four opportunities.

Video response within site search results. Companies have a long way to go in perfecting the basic site search, but one opportunity is to use video-based responses. If a consumer does a search for "safety" on an automaker's site, for example, the results page could link directly to a video of the CEO or another trusted figure walking through the company's safety standards.

FAQ databases. Similarly, FAQ databases should make better use of video responses. Right now, virtually all FAQ databases on corporate sites are grounded in text only.

Feedback forms. Should every feedback form or "contact us" link have a video of the head of customer relations conveying how sincere she is about getting the forms back? It may not be a requirement, but think about how the Kashi brand conveys a "we're listening" mind-set by doing just that.

External search. Brands should buy text ads, on the major search engines that link directly to the video responses when consumers type in a negative term, like "bad service" or "unsafe."

Dear CEO . . .

Like it or not, when consumers have a problem, many of them choose to take it straight to the top. And with all the new CGM vehicles available, it's never been easier for a consumer not only to send a message directly to a CEO but to spread that message to the masses as well—whether by posting a letter of complaint on a blog (as Jeff Jarvis did), recording a video message and putting it on YouTube, or even copying an angry message to an entire extended social network.

But sometimes, even happy customers tell 3,000. That's why it is so critical for CEOs to listen and respond to the concerns—no matter how trifling they may seem—of individual consumers.

For example, when a Bank of America customer service rep gave a man named Travis erroneous information about his account that resulted in a $280 overdraft charge, Travis wrote directly to Bank of America CEO Kenneth Lewis, then sent that same letter to Consumerist.com. A mere twenty-four hours after Lewis received the letter, Travis got a call from an "executive customer service representative" at the bank, who immediately offered to refund the $280. Travis wrote about the happy outcome to Consumerist.com, where his posting received over twelve hundred views and prompted a surprising amount of positive CGM for Bank of America.[5]

In a similar lesson about the importance of CEO responsiveness, in June 2007, a regular named Andy was denied an iced Venti raspberry soy mocha at a local Starbucks. So he wrote an angry letter to none other than the CEO, Howard Schultz and within twenty-four hours received an e-mail from a senior vice president, apologizing for the incident and promising to send him a gift card. Andy wrote to Consumerist .com about how pleased he was with Starbucks's response; his posting received over eleven thousand views and soon found its way to the heavily trafficked Starbucks Gossip blog. With a simple two-line e-mail and a gift card, Starbucks turned a single customer's complaint into a boon of genuine and positive buzz.[6]

When responding to consumers, the CEO and senior managers also need to be sensitive about creating the perception of treating certain key influencers differently than all other consumers. Special treatment can introduce new, unanticipated costs to the firm. If "responsiveness" is exercised selectively, or only against the "squeaky wheel," corporate credibility is put at risk, because consumers will view the gesture as merely a Band-Aid solution. Corporate leaders need to develop smart and relevant responses to consumers but to do so consistently, without setting unrealistic expectations. Dell, for example, in responding to the übermegaphone Jeff Jarvis's public rants about his purportedly dysfunctional laptop, retooled many of its customer service practices for the benefit of *all* Dell customers—not just the most vocal ones.

As a CEO or high-ranking executive, you probably don't have the time to respond personally to each and every customer letter or call. Nevertheless, any and every effort you can make to respond directly, genuinely, and respectfully to unhappy consumers (particularly if they are CGM influencers) will ultimately be rewarded.

Keeping It Real: Authenticity Versus Organizational Growth

Historically, Starbucks has enjoyed a great deal of positive CGM, in large part thanks to its founder and chairman, Howard Schultz's commitment to the ultimate authentic coffee experience. Schultz not only focuses on product quality and customer service but seeks to re-create an authentic global espresso bar culture and offers diverse and delicious coffee products from around the world. As he was recently quoted as saying in *BusinessWeek,* the "one common thread to the success of these marketing stories and the company itself is that they have to be true—and have to be authentic." If you looked at Starbucks's Credibility Quadrant, you'd see great product, great experience, and great service boxes all flashing in the upper-right section.

Recent buzz on Starbucks, however, has been spotty at best. Many have written and posted online that the Starbucks experience (if not the coffee) has become diluted. In response, Howard Schultz wrote a memo (which, in typical CGM fashion, leaked to Starbucks Gossip) warning senior managers that rapid growth threatened to undermine perceptions of authenticity and to commoditize the Starbucks brand. "We have had to make a series of decisions that, in retrospect, have [led] to the watering down of the Starbucks experience," Schultz said. "Removing the original espresso machines removed much of the romance and theatre that was in play."

So what happened to Schultz's original, authentic vision? One challenge for today's businesses is the fact that authenticity is often compromised by competing demands from consumers. In the case of Starbucks, it seems that customers' desire for fast service trumped the desire for the authentic experience, prompting the company to replace the espresso machines with faster automatic machines in all its stores. As Starbucks's global head of product development, Michelle Gass, explained in a Reuters interview: "Our customers have helped lead us to where we are today. They want their beverage in under three minutes." And because faster machines meant Starbucks baristas could serve more customers in a shorter time, the change was a no-brainer in terms of improving efficiency and profit. But at what cost?

The hard question for Starbucks, or any major company in high-growth mode, is when do the operational imperatives of growth compromise credibility? What is a CEO to do when the demands of the company's most devoted CGM evangelists—the ones who provide lots of free advertising through online video and blogs and create highly visible sites like Starbucks Gossip—begin to conflict with policies and initiatives its leadership knows to be more profitable?

Influencers and evangelists may push agendas that are either unrealistic or steeped in a romanticized vision of the company as a mom-and-pop store. However, such influencers can put companies in the delicate position of having to balance the demands of their core customers over the interests of their shareholders. Against this backdrop, the CEO needs to figure out how to be responsive to consumers without sacrificing operational efficiency or profit. This tenuous balance will sometimes lead to conflicts, but credibility still accrues to firms that are grounded in consistent principles and values. Starbucks has never compromised on coffee quality—an unwavering commitment since the first store opened—but has shown a willingness to compromise on harvesting methods. Chick-fil-A's core values include the religious belief that they should never be open on Sunday, but they make up for lost revenues by being one of the highest-satisfaction brands in the fast-food industry.

Chief executive officers like Nike's Mike Parker have shown that it *is* possible to stay authentic while driving profits and growth. Fearing that Nike, a company that has grown from the $8,000-a-year brainchild of the legendary track and field coach Bill Bowerman to a sports and fitness giant with 29,000 employees, net revenues of $15 billion, and operations on six continents, was no longer perceived as "authentic" by certain groups of core consumers, Parker set out to restore credibility with one such group—skateboarders. So he started an entirely new skateboarding division and hired the hippest young new skaters to represent it. With help from his team of skating experts, he then rolled out a brand-new shoe—the Dunk—designed specifically for skateboarding. Although Nike is still, to some extent, plagued by the stigma of being too "corporate," Parker's efforts have gone a long way in keeping the company authentic—and credible—within skateboarding culture.[7]

As firms grow, certain credibility drivers like "authenticity" may be harder to fulfill. The CEO needs to figure out how to pursue operational and fiduciary imperatives of growth while still appearing real, sincere, and credible. One of the best ways of doing this is by appealing directly to consumers in the ways I've described, through video or podcasting, or merely speaking to consumers via a blog. The GM vice president Bob Lutz hasn't compromised one bit of the growth and operational needs of his firm, but by actively participating in the company's blog and communicating to key constituencies in a far more effective and meaningful manner, he manages to sustain an image of authenticity.

My final advice for CEOs is simple: Keep minding your credibility drivers, and never stop monitoring CGM along the way. More than ever before, consumers are volunteering a wealth of real-time insight, much of which can be served right to CEOs' desktops in the form of a simple CGM analysis. Studying CGM is possibly the most efficient and effective way to monitor the health of your corporation or brand. Doing so also nicely positions you to participate in the conversation, which can only win you points in credibility and consumer loyalty.

Chapter 8

The Neglected Stepchild: Consumer Affairs

n January 2006, Paul M. English decided he'd had enough. Enough time listening to smooth jazz while on hold on a customer service line. Enough wrangling with those stupid interactive voice-response systems that never recognize a word the caller is saying. Enough time wasted waiting for a tinny, digital voice to recite an endless stream of options for where to direct a call but never letting the caller get to a live operator or representative. So what did Paul English do? He figured out the private codes for a number of companies that could break through the voice-response systems and get the caller straight to a live operator. Then he compiled a list and posted it on his blog.

The list was an instant hit. Such a hit, in fact, that he received a million visitors to his blog in a single month; was asked to appear on MSNBC, NPR, BBC; and was profiled in *People* magazine. Soon, hundreds of other frustrated consumers began writing him in support of his crusade and sending him more codes.

So Paul English decided to put his newfound celebrity to good use. He founded a movement called Get Human, which he describes as "an all-volunteer effort to improve the lamentable state of present day telephone customer service." His Web site, Gethuman.com, now hosts a database that rates over five hundred companies on the quality of their customer service lines and provides each company's secret code for breaking through to a live operator.[8]

But consumers shouldn't have to hack into a company's voice-automated system to be heard. As we've seen, just listening to what consumers are saying pays huge dividends in both customer loyalty and valuable feedback. If managers, executives, and marketers would only look to their customer service (also called consumer affairs) departments, they'd find a trove of feedback from empowered and vocal consumers that should be harnessed to the fullest.

Clearly, however, not all companies realize this. In fact, customer service and consumer affairs departments hold some of the most underutilized sources of information companies have. I often think of the consumer affairs department as the neglected stepchild of the organization. It's usually stereotyped as a nonstrategic backwater, where troublemaking consumers direct unfounded complaints, outrageous requests, and irrational concerns.

But this isn't the case. In fact, consumer affairs is one of the most important components of credibility. So one of the most critical imperatives for management seeking top-line growth is to rethink, and in many cases reengineer, the entire consumer affairs operation. In fact, this revamping may prove to be a far more efficient, high-return investment than pouring more money into paid media. In an era of affirmation through search results, the stakes for consumer affairs are enormously high.

After all, the consumers most likely to fill out an online feedback form or call the customer service number are the same folks who create online word of mouth. This isn't conjecture. In every study I've conducted on online consumer behavior, a strong correlation exists between consumers who exercise feedback channels and those who create media. In one study, for example, I found that bloggers are almost three times more likely to post comments or provide feedback on a company Web site than are non-bloggers.

Case in point: If you Google the words "Verizon" and "service," you'll receive approximately 33 million results. If you add the word "customer" to the search, nearly 11 million hits remain. The results are not terribly dissimilar for Sony, Sprint, Philips, or any number of major brands. For example, the combined terms "pissed" and "service" and "Ford" yield 1.3 million hits. In other words, an enormous amount of CGM is on the topic of consumer affairs, and most of it is harsh and critical. In fact, consumer affairs generates more unwelcome media than any other arm of a company.

This is why every employee involved in consumer affairs— from the in-store sales staff to the tech support team and the

800-number customer service representatives—plays an integral role in minimizing negative and fostering positive CGM. Remember, highly satisfied consumers turn into brand ambassadors.

Consumer Affairs and the Feedback Pipeline

In order to get a close-up look at what people really think about their businesses or products, companies should immediately start thinking about how to extract more value from the feedback gathered by consumer relations. Here are five ways to jump-start this process.

1. MAKE YOUR CALL-CENTER LINES AS USER-FRIENDLY AS POSSIBLE.

As we saw in the case of Paul English, the inability to get through to a live person on a call-center or customer service line provokes intense frustration—and a whole lot of negative CGM. What's more, consumers can't give feedback if they can't even get through to someone; think about all the useful comments and suggestions that never reach a company because the caller can't get past the automated system and gives up. Give consumers an option to speak to a live representative right away, and have enough representatives on duty that callers don't get stuck on hold for longer than a few minutes. This may mean hiring more people to answer the phones, but your company will reap vast benefits in consumer satisfaction and useful feedback.

2. BEEF UP THE CONSUMER-PROFILING PROCESS.

The majority of the questions on consumer profiling on company feedback forms address mere demographics, such as age, income level, and gender, but not depth of influence—which is much more important in gauging the broader impact of consumers' feedback. Though background information is useful to some extent, in order to assess range of influence, companies should include questions about online behaviors, such as these: "Are you active on Internet forums (if yes, which forums? How often? Do you post text, images, video, audio, or all four)?" "Do you blog?" "Do you have a page on Facebook or MySpace?"

Consider a consumer with a complaint about sanitary conditions at a fast-food restaurant. What's more important to know about this person: his age or the fact that he has a blog and posts frequently on YouTube? If the issue has the potential to generate bad publicity for your company, you'll want to know the consumer's potential to spread the word. The same principle applies in reverse. If a consumer raves about the new Philips flat-screen television, would your company rather know her annual income or the fact that she regularly writes product reviews on Amazon.com and Epinions.com?

3. WARM UP THE WEB SITE INTERFACE.

Make sure your Web site feedback interfaces are as inviting as possible. The feedback forms should be worded in a way that makes consumers feel their opinions truly matter to the company. I'll tell you for free that most Web site feedback interfaces are off-putting. Feedback tools, like advertising, should always try to deepen an emotional connection. You want to replicate the feeling customers have when they walk up to a warm, responsive concierge at a four-star hotel. Cold and impersonal site interfaces, such as McDonald's, inhibit the customer's natural desire to provide feedback. The more hoops you make customers go through, the less likely they're going to be to take the time to offer their opinions.

4. DON'T BURY THE FEEDBACK FORM.

Unfortunately, feedback forms are often pushed down to a Web site's unreachable depths. And if customers can't find such forms right away, they're apt to take their complaints or comments elsewhere—to a place like Consumerist.com, for example, where they do a lot more damage. Like Unilever's Dove brand, for example, invite feedback on the front page of your Web site, not one that is hard to find. This move will yield valuable information—and it's far less expensive than hiring an agency.

5. MAKE SURE YOUR FEEDBACK SYSTEM ACCOMMODATES HOW YOUR CUSTOMERS COMMUNICATE.

Often, consumer affairs is totally out of sync with how consumers express themselves. Consumers today routinely communicate with photos, audio, video, links, and more. If consumers want to write, call, e-mail, send a video, forward a URL, or provide a personal podcast, make sure your company's Web site can accept the format. This is what 360 listening is all about.

Consumer Affairs and the Call Center: One Big Happy Family

If a company truly wants to build trust with its customers, it's important that everyone involved in serving them—from the in-store service reps and the people answering the 800 line to the engineers who develop the automated online service—knows what the others are doing. Here's what can happen if they don't.

In January 2007, a college student named Shane had a maddening experience trying to rent a U-Haul to move himself into his dorm. When he first called U-Haul to make his reservation, he spoke with a very helpful customer service rep who quoted him a price of $225. However, when he arrived the next day to pick up the vehicle, the rep behind the counter told him he owed $480. When he questioned the charge, he was told a branch manager was unavailable to speak with him; he had no choice but to swallow the extra $255.

Unfortunately, Shane's woes didn't end there. When he prepared to move out of his dorm at the end of the semester, he reserved a U-Haul truck again, this time using the online reservation system. But when his father went to pick up the vehicle, the branch didn't even have the truck that had been reserved, and the rep behind the counter claimed that, since the reservation had been made online, he was unable to help. So Shane called the customer service call center, but this rep, too, claimed to be powerless, since the reservation system was automated. Shane's father ended up driving forty-five minutes to pick up a truck at another location, and both swore they would never patronize U-Haul again.

But this wasn't enough for Shane. He was mad and felt it was his duty to let others know just how unhelpful U-Haul's on-site customer service, 800 line, and online reservation system had been. So he began to campaign against the company and posted a letter to Consumerist.com about his experience. His post received over fourteen hundred page views and dozens of sympathetic comments, resulting in a major hit to U-Haul's reputation.

The moral: Make sure that one hand knows what the other is doing. In our online world, the number of channels through which consumers can reach companies is only increasing. This makes it even more important that each and every person involved in customer service be in sync.

Consumer Affairs and Others Within the Organization: A Seat for the Neglected Stepchild at the Dinner Table

If trusted expression is the new currency, breaking down the barriers between consumer affairs and the rest of the company is worth its weight in gold. At the end of the day, explained Beth Thomas-Kim of Nestlé, "consumer affairs is the proxy for consumers when the consumer cannot be there." What could have more broad use and application within the company than that?

Here are six ways your consumer affairs department can forge effective partnerships with other arms of the organization.

1. Sales

A main reason consumers call or write to a consumer affairs department is to find out where to buy a product. Consumer affairs can support sales by either identifying a need—whether it's for more retail locations or branches in a region or more coverage by sales reps in a certain sector—or providing customers the information they need to take to their local store in order to locate an item.

2. Product Development

Consumer affairs can be the first-line defense when there are problems with your product. In the event of a product flaw, defect, or even a recall, make sure your consumer affairs reps are aware of it—and of what you are doing to rectify the problem. That way, when customers call to complain, your reps will have all the information they need to pacify the angry mobs.

But the communication between consumer affairs and product developers shouldn't just flow in one direction. Unmet consumer needs are described to consumer affairs reps every day; when they receive this feedback from customers—whether a product isn't working properly or is flawed in its design—they should have channels to pass this information directly to the people in charge of fixing the problem. Since the consumers who provide feedback tend to be highly attentive to detail, they serve as an invaluable resource to product development, especially for detailed, qualitative feedback.

3. Legal Relations and Risk Management

People who work in consumer affairs are often the first to hear about issues that could lead to litigation. So make sure that your consumer affairs reps have a way to—confidentially, of course—communicate these issues to your company's legal team, so potential liabilities can be handled before they escalate.

4. Market Research

Market research exists to figure out what consumers really want. Consumer affairs can help them find out by polling callers or inviting them to focus groups. How many times have you called consumer affairs to report a problem and then been asked if you'd like to take part in a brief survey? Maybe you didn't opt to participate, but plenty of people do, and their responses are market research gold.

5. Human Resources

Consumers constantly call or write to consumer affairs with comments—both positive and negative—about their experiences with company employees—from cashiers through branch managers to service technicians. This puts consumer affairs in a position to inform human resources about how employees are being perceived by consumers. This data can also help identify gaps in employee training and help HR departments develop better training, incentive, or employee recognition programs.

6. Packaging and Design

Consumer affairs can help ensure that packaging information is clear and accurate, and that critical information, such as best by dates or manufacturing codes, is legible and easily found. For example, if your company sells a packaged food item and people are constantly calling consumer affairs to ask about its calorie or fat content, your package designers should be made aware that this information is either missing or too hard to find.

Good News—The Consumer Affairs Department Is Ready for Web 2.0

Last fall I was invited to Palm Springs by the Society of Consumer Affairs Professionals (SOCAP) to deliver a keynote entitled "Wake Up and Listen to Consumer 2.0." As I prepared my keynote, it became obvious to me that when it comes to a genuine, passionate commitment to consumer listening, consumer affairs is truly ready to step up to the plate.

In fact, before my speech, SOCAP had conducted a survey of all the conference attendees and found that the vast majority of consumer affairs departments are already starting to formally or informally monitor consumer-generated media. Over half indicated that they planned to overhaul their feedback interfaces, nearly half had plans to experiment with blogs, and over a third indicated that they intended to start profiling consumers based on "influence" considerations. And, over 25 percent said they even planned to allow consumers to submit video, audio, or photo feedback.

This is a far cry from the attitude I witnessed in the early days of PlanetFeedback.com, when folks from consumer affairs thought I was crazy for creating a model that so explicitly acknowledged, embraced, and channeled consumer power. But today the empowered consumer is front and center in the consumer affairs viewfinder, and companies appear more than ready for the necessary change.

But consumer affairs can't go it alone. What's most needed right now is a collaboration—in terms of both operations and budget—between the marketing and advertising departments, the CEO, and the consumer affairs department. Reforming consumer affairs to create a more genuine, credible listening infrastructure will require investment, attention, commitment, and engagement throughout the organization.

Now is the time for companies to ask hard questions about whether reallocating or shifting dollars from paid media and advertising to consumer affairs makes sense. And I suspect that in most cases the answer will be that it does. As empirical evidence across the CGM landscape has made clear, making the extra effort and investment in areas like customer service rewards companies generously in credibility, consumer loyalty, and business results.

Chapter 9

When Your Company Is Googled: Troubleshooting

L et's face it. Sooner or later, your company is going to get into trouble. It's just a fact of life that corporations sometimes miscalculate or screw up, unwittingly putting themselves at risk for damaging consumer-generated media. Sometimes they get attacked for justifiable reasons; other times, they are merely convenient targets. Corporate credibility is under fire all the time, and it's harder than ever for corporations to defend themselves. The unmistakable reality in the age of CGM is that the time companies have to respond to a crisis, rumor, or gaffe is a fraction of what it was in the past. Today, bad buzz spreads so quickly that the old let's-wait-until-the-morning approach no longer applies. In our brave new world of one-click information, a CEO can go to bed on top of the world and awake in the morning buried under the rubble of his company's formerly pristine reputation.

But that is no reason to despair. There are a host of steps you can take to defend and protect your company in times of crisis. The more grounded in credibility drivers your company already is, the more effective your troubleshooting will be. After all, companies that are trusted, transparent, authentic, positively affirmed, and good listeners and responders consistently weather storms better than those that are not. But troubleshooting requires a far more strategic and tactical plan than merely hiring a PR or communications firm to "solve the problem." Today, every part of your company plays a role in protecting, defending, and rebuilding your credibility in times of trouble. The following "Troubleshooting Playbook" is meant to offer tips that every arm of an organization can use in a credibility crisis.

The Troubleshooting Playbook

1. KNOW YOUR INFLUENCERS.

As we have seen, influencers are no longer just traditional journalists, financial analysts, or activists. They are now a broader group of average, everyday consumers. To defend your corporate reputation in the era of CGM, you need to pinpoint key influencers as well as understand the scope of consumers' influences. You can't manage a crisis unless you understand who is driving it.

For example, I keep a short list of key influencers who disproportionately impact Nielsen Online's reputation, like people working for other analytics firms or certain marketing bloggers. Your lineup of key influencers will depend on what aspect of business you want to read. Wal-Mart, for example, often attacked in the media for treatment of its employees, keeps an eye on activist groups like Wal-Mart Watch and Wake Up Wal-Mart, which are the first to call the company out for laying off workers, cutting benefits, and so on. And companies sensitive about how they are perceived by environmentalists pay particular attention to groups like As You Sow, which is known for aggressively pushing shareholder resolutions on a host of environmental topics.

Pay attention to Wikipedia.

One excellent strategy for quickly pinpointing influencers and/or issues you may not be aware of is to take a look at your company's entry on Wikipedia, if it has one. Because Wikipedia is the product of hundreds of user contributions, key influencers who circle your corporation are sure to be referenced there. In the McDonald's entry, for example, there's a section dedicated to "criticism," which lists both the issues being debated and the key influencers, like Morgan Spurlock, the flamethrowing director of *Super Size Me*; Eric Schlosser, author of the book *Fast Food Nation*; and activists who have brought legal action against the company.

Given Wikipedia's extraordinary reach—more than a third (36 percent) of American adult Internet users consult it, according to a 2007 Pew Internet study—and the frequency with which entries are updated, Wikipedia is a good reflection of the most relevant issues surrounding your company or brand at any given time. Thus, corporations need to be prepared to address and clarify anything found in their Wikipedia definitions. Since anyone, technically speaking, can make a contribution to Wikipedia, companies can take a crack at editing their own entries to clarify a rumor or respond to an issue. However, if this is done dishonestly, or if the revision veers into shilling or advertising, you can expect a major backlash, deletion of the content, and loss of credibility, as Anheuser-Busch learned the hard way in August 2007, when it was caught red-handed editing criticism about one of its holdings, SeaWorld, in its Wikipedia entry. This is why Dell has a policy that when employees write about the company online—whether on Wikipedia, MySpace, or a personal blog—they have to identify themselves as employees of the company.

A safer way to address criticism in a Wikipedia entry is to do so elsewhere online—whether on the company Web site, a corporate blog, or an activist site like Consumerist.com. Chances are, your response will be spotted and the message spread by an objective third party.

How to Monitor Your Company's Wikipedia Entry

Accuracy: Is the description of your company's policies, practices, and products correct? Is it consistent with the way the company or brand defines itself on its Web site?

Frame of Reference: From what point of view is the story being told? Is the information impartial and objective? Is the story dominated by flamethrowers or detractors?

Points of Reference: What sources are cited? Are they reputable? Are they high exposure? Are they linked to high-exposure

---

sources? Is content on your company Web site being cited? If not, why not?

New News: How quickly are new events being incorporated into the entry? Is your company helping to shape the story by making sure news of new products and initiatives is included?

Look in your own backyard.

Don't overlook the power your loyal advocates have as influencers. Profile your core consumers and keep track of their span of influence. You never know when you may need to galvanize them. If, through smarter profiling, a corporation knows who within its opt-in database qualifies as an influencer, it will be in a much better position to make smart interventions when trouble or challenges erupt.

I recall consulting with a major personal hygiene brand when a false rumor suggesting one of its products had harmful adverse effects was flying all over the Web. The rumor just wouldn't die because it seemed quite credible on the surface, and the company couldn't pinpoint its origins. I convinced my client to start profiling its most loyal consumers on how they use and create CGM. Our profiling technique was rather simple. We simply asked those consumers "How active, if at all, are you on online message boards, forums, or blogs?" and listed a range of options from "every day" to "not at all." Consumer affairs representatives then contacted the individuals whose responses indicated they were high influencers and used this moment of live contact to educate them about the truth. This effort increased the odds that these more vocal consumers would go out of their way to defend the company if the issue were raised; essentially, it created a grassroots team of consumers to quickly address and quash the rumor. In this instance, the company nurtured trust through direct contact, and this contact set the stage for consumers to effectively communicate with other consumers.

Every corporation should have such a team on hand. And again, understand the key questions you need to ask to ensure you are leveraging the right consumers.

2. MAXIMIZE YOUR CORPORATE BLOG.

Corporate blogs are especially useful as a first line of counterattack against unfounded claims. Companies like GM, Toyota, Hewlett-Packard, and IBM are increasingly using their blogs as rapid-response vehicles when thorny issues arise in the media or among bloggers. If you've screwed up, use your blog as a platform to apologize; if you haven't, use it to clarify and defend your actions. The key is to keep the corporate blog credible; CGM culture will sniff out the slightest manipulation.

Corporate Blog Troubleshooting Basics

R*eview, review, review.* In times of crisis, repeat the blog's mission statement every so often to remind consumers what you stand for. Also, remember that new visitors to the blog may not always take the time to scroll down and read earlier posts.

Personalize the blog. Put a face in front of the content, and effuse personality. Angry consumers will be more likely to forgive a company that comes across as human.

Don't be shy. If controversy erupts, the corporate blog is a good place to start defending yourself, or to start apologizing. Customers respond well when a company admits a misstep and takes action to publicize the correction.

Brag—but not too much. Blog about your company's good or significant deeds, strengths, and benefits, but do so without making it seem like a self-serving advertisement. When you've screwed up, it doesn't hurt to remind consumers of all the good things you stand for.

3. Exploit all touch points.

It is important for a company to ensure that all its touch points, in other words, everyone in the organization who has contact with customers—from consumer affairs and sales representatives to the receptionists at company headquarters—has the essential data in hand to defend the company or correct bad information. So make sure that all the following touch points are tuned in to any negative information being spread about the company and be ready with a response.

Use human resources.

Human resources is the department responsible for making sure that employees in all other departments have the tools and training necessary to do their jobs, since a company's credibility is eroded if, for example, a sales representative is unaware of a wildly negative viral video on YouTube. This is why employee training is paramount. Make sure your human resources department offers ample and frequent opportunities for each and every employee to learn about any negative issues or accusations facing the company—and what to do when confronted with them. Everyone who works for you should be prepared to get down in the trenches to defend your company when necessary.

Use the customer service channel.

If your company is being hit by negative CGM, your consumer affairs or customer service department can be your number one front for defense. Post a video on your Web site's feedback page of an executive addressing the controversial issue, or replace the hold music on your 800 line with a detailed recorded message providing assurance about a given problem. You may even want to have customer service reps contact certain high-influence consumers directly (remember the Bank of America story in Chapter 7?). As we've seen, responsiveness is absolutely critical in managing potentially damaging issues.

Use the sales force.

Your sales team can also be a valuable ally in correcting an unfounded rumor or diffusing an attack on your credibility. For better or worse, consumers put an enormous amount of trust in salespeople—after all, these are the folks who know the ins and out of the products. If you are an electronics manufacturer weathering negative buzz about a glitch in a portable DVD player, for example, your sales reps can be indispensable in spreading the word that the glitch has been fixed in the newest model. Of course, when the company has a genuine problem, it's critical that these sales representatives, in order to maintain their own credibility, always dish out the absolute truth.

Use the entire Web.

Bruce Ertmann, Toyota's corporate manager of CGM, spends at least 30 percent of his day surfing the Internet on sixteen computer monitors in his office, frequenting a number of car enthusiast sites, including Autoblog, Jalopnik, and Autoextremist. He contributes to those sites and addresses misleading information about Toyota whenever and wherever it appears. To stay credible while doing so, Ertmann follows three crystal-clear rules:

Transparency: He identifies himself as a representative of Toyota USA in all postings. There is nothing to be gained from secrecy and everything to lose if one of the posts backfires. Ertmann adheres to what he calls "a code of conduct. We aren't consumers and when we drop in," he says, "we can't pretend we are."

Authority: Members of these enthusiast sites have gotten to know Ertmann through his posts and have come to view him as an expert on the car industry. In July 2007, for example, Toyota received what could have been some unfortunate publicity when Al Gore's son was caught going 100 miles an hour in a Prius. Ertmann quickly wrote, "We don't advocate traveling at 100 mph on our nation's highways, or anywhere for that matter in any of our products, but we've also heard from some of our Prius owners that say it's kind of nice to know the car is not a slug at all but has the power to move fast if needed. Just what is the top speed of a Prius? It's actually 103 mph. Buy a Prius—but obey the law."

Competency: Ertmann makes sure that all his claims are well researched and grounded in fact. As a result, he comes across as informed, organized, and competent. When Toyota launched its Tundra truck, for example, it knew it was going into a very competitive market that could get nasty. And it did. So Ertmann gathered information about Tundra and the competing products, produced a fact sheet, and created a separate blog that could be used to provide comparative information to help Toyota dealers. "It's one more way we can stay up on things going around, and the blog is a great tool to get the facts straight," he wrote.

Try advertising by paid search.

Paid search is another smart way of dealing with a crisis. This includes purchasing negative keywords to ensure the company's side of the story is always available to angry consumers. For example, millions of e-mails have circulated around the Web suggesting that ingesting hand sanitizer triggers alcohol poisoning. Online ad networks are getting so sophisticated and ubiquitous, companies can now easily buy exposure on all the top blogs and other areas where consumers may be most likely to learn about an issue. Yet not one of the major hand sanitizer manufacturers has bought any search advertising in an effort to get its side of the story across, so when you type "hand sanitizer" and "safety" into Google, evidence affirming the rumor dominates the results. Turns out, the accusations are true, but makers of the brands would be wise to buy search terms and use them to clarify the fact that sanitizers are dangerous only if large quantities are ingested, and to point out that hand sanitizer is not meant to be ingested in the first place. My advice to brands like Purell and Gojo would be to buy negative key words such as "alcohol poisoning" or "health risks" on search engines so that when consumers search those terms, they get the full picture.

Try to anticipate and dispel consumer concerns before they strike. After all, just seeing a "Get the Real Facts" banner or text ad can provide consumers with some measure of confidence that all is not rotten in the state of Denmark. Sandbag the apprehension, and claim the credit for helping consumers get the best possible information. I refer to this as "curiosity catching."

4. WHEN AN APOLOGY IS NOT ENOUGH.

When your company is under attack, mere apology and clarification may not be enough, especially when consumers are really angry and feel betrayed. In these cases, there's only upside in treating consumers with extra attention, more time, and perhaps even compensation (like JetBlue did for the passengers it left stranded on the runway in February 2007 or, on a smaller scale, like Starbucks did by sending the disgruntled Andy a gift card). Remember, if an unsatisfied consumer does tell 3,000 friends, or even a fraction of that number, one person's experience can carry a real cost. And if the complaint lands on search engine results, that complaint might just become a permanent stain on your company's reputation. It's worth the extra time and resources to turn that single unsatisfied customer into a satisfied one. If it costs a few hundred dollars in a rebate or refund to prevent someone from putting a viral video on YouTube, for example, consider this a relatively cheap form of insurance.

Troubleshooting in Action

When contemplating disasters that might befall your company, it's always instructive to examine how other businesses have weathered the storm. Let's look at three case studies.

Executive Summary

R*espond to complaints.* Treat every complaint as an early warning of a broader, more public attack on the brand. Dissect it, source it, understand it! Consider your response as carefully as you would an advertisement.

Anticipate consumer curiosity. If your company is in trouble or under attack, consider whether curious consumers might try to search for more info. If so, how, where, and when will they find something even more damning? Whatever bad news there is, put it out in the open. Remember, the damage won't be as great if they hear it from you first.

Serve the seekers. When the company is at risk, share any fresh news that might be relevant to consumer needs. Make sure you've got sufficient content and utility on your Web site to answer any questions consumers might be asking.

Blank the blanks. Make sure your company search engine doesn't fire blanks when consumers type in negative terms. A company that doesn't even have a link to an FAQ page when someone searches for "complaint" on its Web site is putting itself in double jeopardy. Make a list of possible negative terms consumers might search for and have answers at the ready.

CASE 1: BRAND UNDER ATTACK

In 2003, the Centre for Science and Environment (an organization in India similar to America's Center for Science in the Public Interest) went after Coca-Cola when it reported discovering high levels of pesticide in Coca-Cola soft drinks.

Almost immediately after CSE put out press releases detailing its findings, sales of Coke products in India dropped by as much as 70 percent, and Coke products were banned in government offices, hospitals, and schools. In an unprecedented move, Coke executives joined with Pepsi execs (who were also named in the CSE press releases) to counter the negative publicity. They went on the offensive, commissioning their own studies, which showed no pesticide residue in their products, then fashioned rebuttals that could be used any time someone questioned the quality of their products.

Unfortunately for them (but instructive for you), Coke underestimated the grassroots nature of the initial report. So, instead of reassuring customers, the technicalities of its overly complicated responses only served to confuse and create more suspicion. Local politicians and NGOs grabbed the issue and ran with it, and the media was soon overwhelmed by claims that Coke products were "toxic." Coke may have erred by relying too much on local media to address the issue, because the activists had a significant leg up in terms of reaching the local TV, radio, and print media. In other words, Coke failed to control the story, and even now the effects of the attack linger in that market.

So what should Coke have done? Setting up a Web site specifically to serve as a knowledge base for concerned consumers would have been an excellent start. That site should have contained detailed yet easy-to-follow explanations of Coke's rebuttal studies, perhaps enhanced by graphics or video clips. The site should have been updated daily, if not multiple times a day, and RSS feeds on all content should have been provided. Remember, when a site is informative, credible, and easy to reference, its content is almost sure to reach and spread through the mainstream media.

CASE 2: PRIVACY SNAFU

America Online was no stranger to publicity fiascos, even before it heard the name Vincent Ferrari. Sometime between March and May 2006, someone in the organization released a file that contained the results of 650,000 searches—many of which were embarrassing or unflattering—that had been performed by AOL users. Though the searches were anonymous, within days of the release, bloggers (with the help of *The New York Times*) were able to piece together the identities of a number of those users and match them with three-month records of all their search queries. Once the breadth of the breach became apparent, AOL pulled the file. But it was too late—thousands of people had already accessed the information. Privacy advocates—not to mention the AOL users—were outraged.

So, how did AOL handle this mess? Not very well, a point even the company conceded in later media interviews. It responded by pushing an unnamed spokesperson to the podium, where he offered a tepid statement about how AOL was "very sorry" this had occurred. That was it. Sure, there were some follow-up statements referencing the possible termination of the person responsible; however, for the most part, the public was left guessing about what had taken place. AOL went on to suffer even more ignominy a short time later with the Vincent Ferrari incident, which merely reinforced perceptions that it put business needs, not the consumer, first.

America Online should have immediately admitted culpability and implemented a new, aggressive policy on privacy issues. Furthermore, it would have done well to offer some form of compensation (even just a month or two of free access) to the users whose privacy had been violated. Then it should have announced—on its Web site and corporate blogs—the steps it was going to take to ensure this didn't happen again.

That's exactly what another Internet company did when faced with a similar crisis. In 2006, the social networking site Facebook ignited outrage after announcing a "news feed" feature that many of its members interpreted as a major breach of privacy. Tens of thousands of Facebook users signed an online petition called "A Day Without Facebook" that noted, among other things:

> It is almost impossible now to keep your information to yourself. In the last year this has become incredibly important as we have seen judicial actions brought against students based solely on photos posted on Facebook, we have heard of cases concerning actual stalking where Facebook was the accused main form of information, and we have seen employers who have begun using Facebook to check on potential employees.

The brouhaha resulted in thousands of news stories about Facebook—the vast majority negative. But Facebook's founder,

Mark Zuckerberg, handled the crisis just right. He listened, quite intently, to the users' comments and within two days posted a heartfelt public apology, showing Facebook users that he had taken their complaints seriously and was making the changes they wanted. He wrote, "We really messed this one up . . . so we have been coding nonstop for two days to get you better privacy controls. This new privacy page will allow you to choose which types of stories go into your Mini-Feed and your friends' News Feeds, and it also lists the type of actions Facebook will never let any other person know about. If you have more comments, please send them over." Almost immediately, the tide of CGM turned—a complete 180—and the angry postings were replaced with grateful ones.

CASE 3: A FLAWED PRODUCT

In September 2006, when a Lenovo laptop exploded at LAX airport, it was discovered that certain Sony batteries used in major brands of laptop computers could combust while in use, triggering one of the biggest product recalls in history. But Lenovo managed the situation by launching a dedicated Web site that included a comprehensive FAQ concerning the recall, plus a user-friendly feature that allowed concerned users to determine quickly whether their laptop batteries were part of the recall. Furthermore, Lenovo erred on the side of caution and extended the recall to batteries in older computers that may or may not have been faulty. The company made no attempt to downplay or minimize the situation or place the blame on Sony (even though Sony had manufactured the batteries); Lenovo simply bit the bullet, took the hit, and got over the snafu quickly, efficiently, and without too much damage to its credibility.

Conclusion: It's Time to Lead—No Excuses

At the end of the day, the single most important thing for managers to do in this age of consumer control is simply lead. But contrary to what some might think, leadership in the age of CGM doesn't necessarily require advanced technical skills, vast computer experience, or superior Web savvy. After all, we are all consumers. We've all raged at a customer service rep over the phone, gotten a little testy with a sales-clerk, and probably even posted a few nasty things about a company online that we may regret. We all sense and feel the changes of the digital age, so it's time to use our instincts and initiative, and put our good judgment into action.

When I look back on my own business experience, I'm most proud of the "off the plan" acts of leadership that deepened my commitment to learning about the new face of marketing. For example, in 1995, fresh out of business school, I was surprised by the lack of internal conversation at Procter & Gamble about the Web and decided to launch an e-mail discussion group, which I called "Net-Net, The Net." I didn't care whether the participants came from marketing, research, IT, sales, or even the intern pool. I wanted to get as many P&Gers as possible sharing, conversing, and engaging about all aspects of the Internet. It was obvious to me that P&G is a company that makes big things happen once the right information gets put on the table. So my e-mail forum became a platform for doing exactly that.

I didn't wait for a research brief, white paper, or "fact book" green light to take action. In some respects, I was just lucky to see an unmet need and fill it before anyone else did. I also didn't let the naysayers (every organization has plenty) slow me down; I was acting on my own intuition.

In a way similar to what's happening in today's social media environment, curious and like-minded folks quickly joined the group, which had grown to over five hundred by the time I left the company. I knew I had acquired a level of power and influence when I received an e-mail from P&G's chief information officer politely asking whether he and four other managers could join my mailing list.

The point is, opportunity is everywhere, and because lines of ownership are so fuzzy these days, everyone's capable of reaping the dividends of small or bold acts of leadership. So whether you are the CEO, a marketing manager, a product developer, a Web designer, or a call-center representative, you can—and should—be questioning whether your company is doing everything it can to stay credible on every front.

Here are some specific questions anyone—regardless of title or position—can bring to the table when the company's credibility is threatened.

ALWAYS LISTEN. Why aren't we listening more attentively to consumers? They are talking all around us—with high-tech megaphones—yet our current approach is absorbing only a slice of that feedback. How can we listen more systematically, to save time, receive a wealth of hints, make better marketing and product decisions, and most important, better understand how to communicate our best attributes?

SHIFT FROM PAID MEDIA TO CONSUMER MEDIA! Why is all our media planning focused on paid media? If word of mouth is the key engine of awareness, why aren't we nurturing great experiences with consumers that will generate more persuasive, credible media? We can do this through improved customer service, world-class Web site experiences, and other forms of relationship marketing, *and* we can save money in the process.

RETHINK CONSUMER AFFAIRS. Why aren't we spending more money on consumer affairs, the new epicenter of relationship marketing? There's plenty of evidence that consumers who rant or rave tell many others beyond our walls, so let's invest in those relationships.

RECOMMEND A NEW POSITION: MANAGER OF CONSUMER-GENERATED MEDIA. It's time to really take action on consumer-generated media. We need thoughtful, experienced managers who know how to listen to and engage consumers. Toyota, *Advertising Age*'s 2006 Marketer of the Year, has a person heading a department dedicated exclusively to consumer-generated media. What can we do that is similar?

WALK THE TALK. We'll never get anywhere in this unpredictable world of CGM unless we have hands-on experience. That way, the whole arena will seem less foreign and more intuitive. Can we set up an internal blog, or perhaps a wiki, so we all can walk the talk on this medium?

EMPOWER THE YOUNGER RANKS. Has anyone noticed how naturally in touch our younger ranks—especially those interns—are with new forms of opinion and expression? Why don't we create a special subcommittee to have them provide strategic and tactical input on how to stay ahead of the curve? No doubt they could teach us new tricks, and we'll keep them motivated and energized in the process.

END THE TIME STAMPS, AND START THE CONVERSATION! Conversations are fluid and provide deeper context and meaning than time stamps. When media measurements are increasingly anchored to online advertising tools, the conversation matters. The focus group we draw from is rarely closed. Let's rethink the way we do research to focus more on real-time conversations, and use them as our new accountability scorecards.

THINK BEYOND LOYALTY. In this age of CGM, customer loyalty is simply not enough. We need to pay more attention to whether loyalty translates into advocacy. We must judge our success on what consumers tell others online. Along the way, we need to carefully monitor whether the residue of their feelings shows up in search results.

REMEMBER, CREDIBILITY MATTERS. Our corporate credibility is fragile in this age of consumer-generated media. We must rethink the way we build it, protect it, and nurture it. In this time of transparency, we can't pull the wool over anyone's eyes. We're the ones being "monitored for quality purposes."

Good luck!

Epilogue

My father passed away last November, shortly after I submitted my final manuscript for *Satisfied Customers Tell Three Friends, Angry Customers Tell 3,000.* It's both painful and difficult to accept that he won't be around for the book release and the conversation I expect it to trigger and catalyze. After all, he helped get the process going in the first place.

My father was an accomplished advertising executive, and my fascination with marketing and advertising undoubtedly stems from my many early childhood visits to the office of his Hollywood-based firm, Eisamann, Johns, and Laws. Indeed, I grew up on ad jingles and storyboards; I especially relished watching the outtakes of commercials he'd bring home, and delighted in the occasional visit to a TV set for a Chevrolet commercial.

A superb listener, my father was an incredible relationship builder, and his personal "brand" was infinitely accessible— and always credible. His memorial service, drawing friends from all corners, reinforced his gifts in a big way. He wasn't perfect, but he was authentic, genuine, trustworthy; in fact, he embodied in a big way all of the checked "Six Drivers of Credibility" I describe in this book, and I owe much to him for steering my own career around marketing and advertising.

When I worked at Procter & Gamble, playing a key role in shaping industry standards around online advertising, my father served as an informal adviser, balancing my exuberance with the new with a faith in the timeless truths of the old. And when I left P&G to take the "consumer side" of the equation vis-à-vis one of the Web's first consumer-generated media experiments, PlanetFeedback, he helped me make the critical connection between consumer opinion and marketing needs.

Of course, his teaching always had broader implications. Attention and engagement, he reminded me, is not merely a scarce commodity in advertising, but something we must earn in every pursuit—and always credibly.

In the weeks before his death, we could spend hours discussing the dynamics and accuracies of *Mad Men*, the AMC television series documenting the often complex lives of Madison Avenue advertising executives in the early 1960s. The firm portrayed in the series was a loose play on BBDO, the very firm where my father launched his own ad career. At one point, I even posted excerpts of his commentary on YouTube.

But let's stop short of over-romanticizing what's often known as the Golden Age of Advertising. The industry was hardly perfect, and often lacking in credibility. (After all, where's credibility in suggesting that smoking cigarettes makes people seem glamorous and sexy?) At the same time, however, many of the lines around advertising were cleaner, and less ambiguous. If the advertiser danced in the gray zone, you usually knew it. Product placement, for example, was far less hidden—often it was so blatant and transparent that it bordered on the absurd—and so many of the other tricks that marketers and advertisers use these days simply didn't exist.

Today, things are far murkier. Ads are everywhere, and with the consumers' limited attention, marketers and advertisers find ourselves scraping for every possible venue for getting the consumers "engagement"—even down to the mobile phone small screen. We glorify the wonders of ad-targeting technology, like click-through ads, that target the right consumer with the right ad at the right time.

Unlike my father's simple marketing tool kit—TV, print, and radio—we now have unlimited choices for getting out the message. And we have access to the consumer—at the most intimate levels, sometimes bordering on encroachment—in ways my father would have never imagined.

But this doesn't necessarily make managing brands any easier. If anything, all of us—marketers, advertisers, managers, all the way up to the top executive—need to think harder and work smarter about how we message to and interact with a new consumer audience that has greater choice, greater control, greater leverage, and greater knowledge of what's really going on around, beneath, and behind the brand. We need to find ways to manage consumers' expectations and to provide service that meets their ever-growing needs.

And trust me, even in the months since I finished this book, the world of advertising and consumer-generated media has hit new obstacles, presented new challenges, and reached new levels of complexity, as consumers are asking even harder questions about everything from the credibility of "green" claims to the ugly side of privacy infringement on social networking sites like Facebook.

And so we must navigate this brave new world with our credibility compass, all the while keeping in mind the very things my father lived, embodied, and emphasized repeatedly, throughout his career and his life.

Pete Blackshaw
January 30, 2008

NOTES

1. Nitasha Tiku, "When Scandal Knocks," *Inc.*, August 2007.

2. Tim Cass, "Not All Fun and Games," *BusinessWeek,* July 9, 2007.

3. Matthew Creamer, "At Last, the Reviews Are In: Wal-Mart Wakes Up to the Power of the People," *Advertising Age,* July 23, 2007.

4. Maha Atal and Conrad Wilson, "Feeling Trashed on the Web? Here's How to Avoid Having Your Brand Message Hijacked," *BusinessWeek,* September 2007.

5. http://consumerist.com/consumer/customer-service/man-gets-280-back-from-bank-of-america-after-writing-ceo-253623.php.

6. http://consumerist.com/consumer/starbucks/epic-battle-for-raspberry-syrup-ends-with-starbucks-apology-and-gift-card-269019.php.

7. Bill Breen, "Who Do You Love?" *Fast Company,* May 2007.

8. William C. Taylor, "Your Call Should Be Important to Us, but It's Not," *New York Times,* February 26, 2006.

INDEX